Is This The Mary Of The Bible?

Is the Mary of Catholicism the Mary of the Bible?

Contents

Introduction

I was raised a Roman Catholic before Vatican Council II and still remember saying, *I'll die a Catholic.* Perhaps this is because of what the priest dogmatically asserted, and **I once believed—that only Roman Catholics will not be damned.** (Maybe he taught this because he was aware of the *ex cathedra* statement in 1302 by Pope Boniface VIII, the *Bull Unam Sanctam*, which states it is *absolutely necessary* for one to be in subjection to the Roman Pontiff for *salvation*.) I also remember him saying, *The difference between Catholics and Protestants is* ***we have Mary and they don't.*** When I look back over the years I realize that 95% of all my friends and family members that I knew at that time were also Roman Catholics.

After I graduated from college, I had an insatiable hunger for *truth*. I wanted some solid facts upon which to live my life and guide me. I had also been humbled because of an injury. These made my heart fertile soil when I started my search. Because neither the priest nor my catechism teachers placed any emphasis on reading the Bible, I never thought of going to the Scriptures! I instead read some of what Confucius wrote, since he was supposed to be a sage. I was disappointed with his writings and felt empty. A woman who worked at a secular book store told me to read the book of *Proverbs* because I asked her where I could find wise saying or proverbs. I remember telling her I never knew the Bible had a section in it called *Proverbs*. Around the same time my mother received a book from someone on TV who wrote that if you read the Bible for three weeks for 15 minutes a day, it will change your life. Hence, I started doing this at about the age of 22 or 23. Since the only Bible I trusted at the time was the Catholic Bible, I read it alone in my quest for *truth*.

I was shocked at what I was seeing. In fact, it was one surprise after another. Reading the Catholic Bible threw me into great confusion at first because not everything I read paralleled what I was taught as stated in the *Baltimore Catechism.*[1] It was slowly starting to dawn on me that not everything I was taught in church was true. One thing really hit me as I read the Bible: How little Mary was emphasized in the New Testament in contrast to how she was exalted by the priest who spoke at mass. Later, I was bothered how the Ten Commandments in Exodus 20 were different from the ones I learned as stated in the *Baltimore Catechism.*

As I continued to read through the New Testament, I was terror struck when I noticed what Jesus taught in Mt. 7:13,14:

Enter through the narrow gate. **For wide is the gate and broad is the road that leads to destruction, and many enter through it.** But small is the gate and narrow the road that leads to life, and **only a few find it.**

This too went against what I was taught. I grew up thinking most people go to Purgatory (and they will eventually get out of there and go to heaven), and very *few* go directly to either heaven or hell. I knew from reading Mt. 7:13,14 that I didn't *love God* enough to be one of the *few* to go to heaven. As I kept reading I came to Lk. 18:9-14. That is where Jesus taught about the sinful man who sincerely prayed, *God have mercy on me a sin-*

---

1   1962 edition.

ner. The Lord said he went home *justified*. **I realized I had never gone directly to God to get my sins forgiven. I had always gone to the priest, as I had been instructed.** I dropped down on my knees and *sincerely* prayed that prayer and repented of all my sins. I also told God I would serve Him in this life and throughout all eternity. It was like a bomb went off inside me. I got off my knees and sat back down and read more of the Bible. On and off for about three days I kept crying and asking God to forgive me for all of my wickedness. I felt so clean and light it is hard to describe.

I stopped praying to Mary and singing praise songs to her, but often received communion. Within the next year five members of my family died (three close relatives and two more distant) and a very close relative got converted into Jehovah's Witnesses. In his zeal and love for my widowed mother, widowed grandmother and me, he drove in from another state to convert us into his new belief system with another JW who was once a Catholic monk. Because my beliefs were so severely challenged by him, I had to get very serious about Bible doctrine. As I did this, I learned more and more. This led to me rejecting both Catholicism and the Jehovah's Witnesses. I finally made my exit from the Catholic church, a move I never regretted, because of a Marian vision. When I made my exit from the RC church, Vatican Council II had already occurred.

To make a long story short, after another five years or so I quit my job, went to Bible school, got ordained and pastored for nearly seven years. I thought I could do more good for God's kingdom by doing evangelistic type work. Consequently, with my wife's dedication, up went our web site with hundreds of articles as well as various booklets and our 801 page exhaustive refutation to the teaching of eternal security, *The Believer's Conditional Security*. (You can visit it at www.evangelicaloutreach. org)

Not too long before I started to pastor, a former Catholic woman testified that she at one time attended a charismatic Catholic church. She went on to say that, at times, people there would prophesy, *thus saith Mary*. Another credible source confirmed this happens in charismatic Catholic circles.

It is my sincere prayer, as a former Catholic who in times past prayed the Rosary and wore the Brown Scapular, that all Catholics will carefully examine, *Is This The Mary of the Bible?* In it you will read: (1) The present-day official position of Catholicism on Mary and (2) What the Bible says about this. **Hundreds of millions of Catholics over the years have believed or are at this moment believing what you are about to read, as taught by Catholic authorities, including the present-day Pope himself. Since all of this is related to *salvation*, your eternal destiny will be affected by what you choose to believe about the *Mary of Catholicism* and these issues.**

As you read this book, you are not reading an attack on the *Mary of the Bible*. This is important to remember. Instead you are being shown that the *Mary of the Bible* is not the *Mary of Catholicism*. These are two totally different people, though each share some common characteristics. May GOD BLESS YOU as you verify all the evidence.

Trusting In Jesus 100% For My Salvation,

Dan Corner

1

The Mary Of Present-Day Catholicism

Much confusion exists regarding the beliefs of present-day Catholicism, especially since Vatican Council II. Since that Council, the Catholic church copyrighted in 1994 their doctrinal thoughts in a volume entitled, *Catechism of the Catholic Church*. In it Pope John Paul II wrote:

> **The *Catechism of the Catholic Church*, lastly, is offered to every individual** who asks us to give an account of the hope that is in us (cf. *1 Pet* 3:15) and **who wants to know what the Catholic Church believes.**[1]

Furthermore, Pope John Paul II wrote the following about its use:

> The *Catechism of the Catholic Church* is the result of very extensive collaboration; it was prepared over six years of intense work done in a spirit of complete openness and fervent zeal.
>
> In 1986, I entrusted a **commission of twelve Cardinals and Bishops**, chaired by Cardinal Joseph Ratzinger,

---

1   *Catechism of the Catholic Church* (Liguori, MO: Liguori Publications, 1994), p. 6.

with the task of preparing a draft of the catechism requested by the Synod Fathers. **An editorial committee of seven diocesan Bishops, experts in theology and catechesis, assisted the commission in its work.**[2]

Therefore, **I ask all the Church's Pastors and the Christian faithful to receive this catechism** in a spirit of communion **and to use it assiduously in fulfilling their mission of proclaiming the faith and calling people to the Gospel life.**[3]

Hence, all teachings found within its pages have the endorsement of the Pope regarding the official teachings of the Roman Catholic Church since Vatican Council II. **The following quotes regarding Mary are all found within this book.** (The number at the beginning of the quote is the paragraph number.)

**Mary was *Redeemed* at the
Point of Her Conception;
Mary was Preserved from Original Sin**

491 Through the centuries the Church has become ever more aware that **Mary, "full of grace" through God, was redeemed from the moment of her conception.** That is what the dogma of **the Immaculate Conception** confesses, as Pope Pius IX proclaimed in 1854:

The Most Blessed Virgin Mary was, from the first moment of her conception, by a singular grace and privilege of almighty God and by virtue of the merits of Jesus Christ, Savior of the human race, preserved immune from all stain of original sin.[4]

---

2   Ibid., p. 3.
3   Ibid., p. 5.
4   Ibid., pp. 123, 124.

Mary Remained Free From Personal Sin

493 The Fathers of the Eastern tradition call the Mother of God "the All-Holy" (*Panagia*) and celebrate her as "free from any stain of sin, as though fashioned by the Holy Spirit and formed as a new creature." **By the grace of God Mary remained free of every personal sin her whole life long.**[5]

Mary was Sinless her Whole Life Through

508 From among the descendants of Eve, God chose the Virgin Mary to be the mother of his Son. **"Full of grace," Mary is "the most excellent fruit of redemption" (SC 103): from the first instant of her conception, she was totally preserved from the stain of original sin and she remained pure from all personal sin throughout her life.**[6]

Mary was Sinless and Co-redemptrix with Christ; Mary was the *Cause* of her own Salvation, as well as the Human Race; We have *Life through Mary*

494 ... Espousing the divine will for salvation wholeheartedly, **without a single sin to restrain her,** she gave herself entirely to the person and to the work of Her Son; she did so **in order to serve the mystery of redemption with him** and dependent on him, by God's grace:

> As St. Irenaeus says, "being obedient **she became the cause of salvation for herself and for the whole human race."** Hence not a few of the early Fathers gladly assert ...: "The knot of Eve's disobedience was untied by Mary's obedience: what the virgin Eve bound through her disbe-

---

5   Ibid., p. 124.
6   Ibid., p. 128.

lief, Mary loosened by her faith." Comparing her with Eve, they call Mary "the Mother of the living" and frequently claim: "**Death through Eve, life through Mary.**"[7]

Mary is *Mother of God*

495 ... In fact, the One whom she conceived as man by the Holy Spirit, who truly became her son according to the flesh, was none other than the Father's eternal Son, the second person of the Holy Trinity. Hence **the Church confesses that Mary is truly "Mother of God"** (*Theotókos*).[8]

Mary was a Perpetual Virgin

499 The deepening of faith in the virginal motherhood led the Church to confess **Mary's real and perpetual virginity** even in the act of giving birth to the Son of God made man. In fact, Christ's birth "did not diminish his mother's virginal integrity but sanctified it." And so the liturgy of **the Church celebrates Mary *Aeiparthenos,* the "Ever-virgin."**[9]

510 **Mary "remained a virgin in conceiving her Son, a virgin in giving birth to him, a virgin in carrying him, a virgin in nursing him at her breast, always a virgin."**[10]

Jesus was Mary's Only Son, but She is the Spiritual Mother of All

501 **Jesus is Mary's only son,** but **her spiritual motherhood extends to all men** whom indeed he came to save: "The Son whom she brought forth is he whom God placed as the first-born

---

7   Ibid., pp. 124, 125.
8   Ibid., p. 125.
9   Ibid., p. 126.
10   Ibid., p. 128.

among many brethren, that is, the faithful in whose generation and formulation she cooperates with a mother's love."[11]

507 At once virgin and mother, **Mary is the symbol and the most perfect realization of the Church:** "the church indeed ... by receiving the word of God in faith becomes herself a mother. By preaching and Baptism she brings forth sons, who are conceived by the Holy Spirit and born of God, to a new and immortal life. She herself is a virgin, who keeps in its entirety and purity the faith she pledged to her spouse."[12]

Mary Cooperated in Human Salvation

511 **The Virgin Mary "cooperated through free faith and obedience in human salvation"** ... **By her obedience she became the new Eve, mother of the living.**[13]

The Church is in Mary

829 "But while **in** the most Blessed Virgin the Church has already reached that perfection whereby she exists without spot or wrinkle, the faithful still strive to conquer sin and increase in holiness. And so **they turn their eyes to Mary":** in her the Church is already the "all-holy."[14]

It is Mother and Son in the Work of Salvation; Mary Joined Herself with Jesus' Sacrifice by Enduring the Intensity of His Suffering

964 Mary's role in the Church is inseparable from her union with Christ and flows directly from it. **"This union of the mother**

---

11   Ibid., p. 127.
12   Ibid., p. 128.
13   Ibid., p. 128.
14   Ibid., p. 220.

with the Son in the work of salvation is made manifest from the time of Christ's virginal conception up to his death"; it is made manifest above all at the hour of his Passion:

> Thus the Blessed Virgin advanced in her pilgrimage of faith, and faithfully persevered in her union with her Son unto the cross. There she stood, in keeping with the divine plan, enduring with her only begotten Son the intensity of his suffering, **joining herself with his sacrifice in her mother's heart,** and lovingly consenting to the immolation of this victim, born of her: to be given, by the same Christ Jesus dying on the cross, as a mother to his disciple, with these words: "Woman, behold your son."[15]

**Mary was Resurrected Bodily
to Heaven as *Queen over all things;*
Mary's Resurrection is a Participation
in Jesus' Resurrection**

966 "Finally **the Immaculate Virgin, preserved free from all stain of original sin, when the course of her earthly life was finished, was taken up body and soul into heavenly glory, and exalted by the Lord as Queen over all things,** so that she might be the more fully conformed to her Son, the Lord of lords and conqueror of sin and death." **The Assumption of the Blessed Virgin is a singular participation in her Son's Resurrection and an anticipation of the resurrection of other Christians.**[16]

---

15   Ibid., p. 251.
16   Ibid., p. 252.

Mary is Co-savior in Restoring
Supernatural Life to Souls

968 Her role in relation to the Church and to all humanity goes still further. "In a wholly singular way **she cooperated by her obedience, faith, hope, and burning charity in the Savior's work of restoring supernatural life to souls. For this reason she is a mother to us in the order of grace.**"[17]

Mary's Intercession From Heaven
Brings Gifts of Salvation;
Mary is Advocate, Helper,
Benefactress, and Mediatrix

969 "This motherhood of Mary in the order of grace continues uninterruptedly from the consent which she loyally gave at the Annunciation and which she sustained without wavering beneath the cross, until the eternal fulfilment of all the elect. **Taken up to heaven she did not lay aside this saving office but by her manifold intercession continues to bring us the gifts of eternal salvation .... Therefore the Blessed Virgin is invoked in the Church under the titles of Advocate, Helper, Benefactress, and Mediatrix.**"[18]

Mary Doesn't Diminish
Christ's Unique Mediation

970 "Mary's function as mother of men in no way obscures or diminishes this unique mediation of Christ, but rather shows its power ...."[19]

---

17   Ibid., p. 252.
18   Ibid., p. 252.
19   Ibid., p. 253.

**Essential to Christian Worship is Devotion to Mary;
The Faithful go to Mary in their
Times of Dangers and Needs;
The Epitome of the Whole Gospel,
the Rosary, Expresses Devotion to Mary**

971 *"All generations will call me blessed"*: **"The Church's devotion to the Blessed Virgin is intrinsic to Christian worship."** The Church rightly honors "the Blessed Virgin with special devotion. From the most ancient times the Blessed Virgin
has been honored with the title of 'Mother of God,' **to whose
protection the faithful fly in all their dangers and needs**....
This very special devotion ... differs essentially from the adoration which is given to the incarnate Word and equally to the
Father and the Holy Spirit, and greatly fosters this adoration."
The liturgical feasts dedicated to the Mother of God and **Marian
prayer, such as the rosary, an "epitome of the whole Gospel,"** express this devotion to the Virgin Mary.[20]

The Church *Venerates* Mary

972 After speaking of the Church, her origin, mission, and destiny, we can find no better way to conclude than by **looking to
Mary**. In her we contemplate what the Church already is in her
mystery on her own "pilgrimage of faith," and what she will be
in the homeland at the end of her journey. There, "in the glory
of the Most Holy and Undivided Trinity," "in the communion of
all the saints," **the Church is awaited by the one she venerates
as Mother of her Lord and as her own mother.**[21]

---

20   Ibid., p. 253.
21   Ibid., p. 253.

Mary Cooperated with
Everything Jesus Accomplished

973 By pronouncing her "fiat" at the Annunciation and giving her consent to the Incarnation, **Mary was already collaborating with the whole work her Son was to accomplish. She is mother** wherever he is Savior and head of the Mystical Body.[22]

Mary Now Shares in the
Glory of her Son's Resurrection

974 **The Most Blessed Virgin Mary, when the course of her earthly life was completed, was taken up body and soul into the glory of heaven, where she already shares in the glory of her Son's Resurrection, anticipating the resurrection of all members of his Body.**[23]

Mary is *Mother of the Church* and Exercises
Her Maternal Role From Heaven

975 **"We believe that the Holy Mother of God, the new Eve, Mother of the Church, continues in heaven to exercise her maternal role on behalf of the members of Christ."**[24]

The Church in Paradise is
Centered Around Jesus and Mary

1053 "We believe that **the multitude of those gathered around Jesus and Mary in Paradise forms the Church of heaven, ...**"[25]

---

22   Ibid., p. 254.
23   Ibid., p. 254.
24   Ibid., p. 254.
25   Ibid., p. 274.

The Prayers and Good Works
Of Mary and the Saints
Attained Their Own Salvation and
Cooperated in the Saving of Others

1477 "This treasury includes as well the prayers and good works of the Blessed Virgin Mary. They are truly immense, unfathomable, and even pristine in their value before God. In the treasury, too, are the prayers and good works of all the saints, all those who have followed in the footsteps of Christ the Lord and by his grace have made their lives holy and carried out the mission the Father entrusted to them. In this way they attained their own salvation and at the same time cooperated in saving their brothers in the unity of the Mystical Body."[26]

Mary is *all-holy,* the *Example of Holiness*
and the *Model* of the Church

2030   ... From the Church he learns the *example of holiness* and recognizes its model and source in the all-holy Virgin Mary .... (italics theirs)[27]

To Improperly use Mary's Name is a Violation
of the Second Commandment Which
Forbids the Abuse of God's Name

2146 The second commandment *forbids the abuse of God's name,* i.e., every improper use of the names of God, Jesus Christ, but also of the Virgin Mary and all the saints.[28]

---

26   Ibid., p. 371.
27   Ibid., p. 490.
28   Ibid., p. 519.

Mary Is Praised Because She Knew The Humanity Which Jesus Espoused

2675 ... In countless hymns and antiphons expressing this prayer, two movements usually alternate with one another: the first "magnifies" the Lord for the "great things" he did for his lowly servant **and through her for all human beings; the second entrusts the supplications and praises of the children of God to the Mother of Jesus, because she now knows the humanity which, in her, the Son of God espoused.**[29]

Catholics Pray To Mary, the *Ark of the Covenant;* Mary is *the Dwelling of God with Men*

2676 This twofold movement of **prayer to Mary** has found a privileged expression in the *Ave Maria* :

> ...Mary, in whom the Lord himself has just made his dwelling, is **the daughter of Zion in person, the ark of the covenant, the place where the glory of the Lord dwells.** She is **"the dwelling of God ... with men."** Full of grace, Mary is wholly given over to him who has come to dwell in her and whom she is about to give to the world.[30]

We Can Entrust our Cares and Petitions to Mary; Mary is the *Mother of Mercy, the All-Holy One;* We are to Surrender "the Hour of our Death" Wholly to Her Care; After Death, [those who enter Paradise] are Led to Jesus by Mary

2677 ... Because she gives us Jesus, her son, Mary is Mother of God and **our mother: we can entrust all our cares and peti-**

---

29   Ibid., pp. 642, 643.
30   Ibid., p. 643.

tions to her: she prays for us** as she prayed for herself: "Let it be to me according to your word." **By entrusting ourselves to her prayer, we abandon ourselves to the will of God together with her: "Thy will be done" .... By asking Mary to pray for us, we acknowledge ourselves to be poor sinners and we address ourselves to the "Mother of Mercy," the All-Holy One.** We give ourselves over to her now, in the Today of our lives. And our trust broadens further, already at the present moment, **to surrender "the hour of our death" wholly to her care.** May she be there as she was at her son's death on the cross. **May she welcome us as our mother at the hour of our passing to lead us to her son, Jesus, in paradise.**[31]

Prayer To Mary is Exalted;
We can Pray With and To Mary

2679 Mary is the perfect *Orans* (pray-er), a figure of the Church. **When we pray to her**, we are adhering with her to the plan of the Father, who sends his Son to save all men. Like the beloved disciple we welcome Jesus' mother into our homes, for she has become **the mother of all the living. We can pray with and to her. The prayer of the Church is sustained by the prayer of Mary** and united with it in hope.[32]

The Church Entrusts Supplications
and Praises To Mary

2682 Because of Mary's singular cooperation with the action of the Holy Spirit, the Church loves to pray in communion with the Virgin Mary, to magnify with her the great things the Lord has done for her, and **to entrust supplications and praises to her.**[33]

---

31 Ibid., pp. 643, 644.
32 Ibid., p. 644.
33 Ibid., p. 644.

38 Facts About *The Mary of Catholicism*

What you are about to read is embraced by hundreds of millions of Catholics all the way up to the Pope himself. These concepts are not just held by a small fringe group, but the majority of Roman Catholics:

1. Mary was *redeemed* at the point of her conception.
2. Mary was preserved from original sin.
3. Mary remained free from personal sin.
4. Mary was sinless and co-redemptrix with Christ.
5. Mary was the *cause* of her own salvation, as well as the human race.
6. We have spiritual *life through Mary.*
7. Mary is *Mother of God.*
8. Mary was a perpetual virgin.
9. James and Joseph were sons of another Mary.
10. Jesus was Mary's only son, but she is the spiritual mother of all.
11. Mary cooperated in human salvation.
12. The Church is in Mary.
13. It is Mother and Son in the work of salvation.
14. Mary joined herself with Jesus' sacrifice by enduring the intensity of His suffering.
15. After her death, Mary was resurrected Bodily in Heaven as *Queen over all things.*
16. Mary's resurrection is a participation in Jesus' resurrection.
17. Mary is co-savior in restoring supernatural life to souls.
18. Mary's intercession from Heaven brings gifts of salvation.
19. Mary is Advocate, Helper, Benefactress, and Mediatrix.
20. Mary doesn't diminish Christ's unique mediation.
21. Essential to Christian worship is devotion to Mary.

22. The faithful go to Mary in their times of dangers and needs.
23. The epitome of the whole gospel, the Rosary, expresses devotion to Mary.
24. The Church *Venerates* Mary.
25. Mary cooperated with everything Jesus accomplished.
26. Mary now shares in the glory of her Son's resurrection.
27. Mary is *Mother of the Church.*
28. The Church in Paradise is centered around Jesus and Mary.
29. The prayers and good works of Mary and the saints attained their own salvation and cooperated in the saving of others.
30. Mary is *all-holy,* the *example of holiness* and *Model* of the Church.
31. To improperly use Mary's name is a violation of the second commandment which forbids the abuse of God's name.
32. Catholics are to pray <u>to</u> Mary, the *ark of the covenant.*
33. We can entrust our cares and petitions to Mary.
34. Mary is the *Mother of Mercy, the All-Holy One.*
35. We are to surrender "the hour of our death" wholly to her care.
36. Prayer to Mary is exalted.
37. We can pray with and <u>to</u> Mary.
38. The Church entrusts supplications and praises to Mary.

Who Am I, According to Present-Day Catholic Beliefs?

1. I am the sinless, All-Holy One, to whom Christians are to pray in dangers and times of need.
2. I was resurrected bodily and the church in Paradise is focused, in part, upon me.

3.   I am the *ark of the covenant* and the dwelling of God with men.
4.   My name, if improperly used, is a violation of the second commandment.
5.   The epitome of the whole gospel expresses devotion to me.
6.   I am an Advocate, Helper, Benefactress, and Mediatrix.
7.   You have *life* through me.
8.   I am to be praised and venerated.
9.   Basic to Christian *worship* is devotion to me.
10.   I was the cause of my own salvation as well as that of the whole human race.
11.   I was redeemed at the point of my conception.
12.   I am the Mother of God, the Mother of Mercies, the ever-virgin Queen of Heaven, the new Eve, the daughter of Zion who Co-operated in the Savior's Work.

(Comment: If you never read the aforementioned official Catholic teachings on Mary, like many, you might have thought the first 9 of these 12 points were describing the Lord Jesus!)

Examining *The Mary of Catholicism*
From a Biblical Perspective

1.   One of the unique glories of God is declared in the following Scripture:

This righteousness from God comes through faith in Jesus Christ to all who believe. There is no difference, for **all have sinned and fall short of the glory of God** (Rom. 3:22,23).

Only God is *sinless,* which includes Jesus, whereas all other people have sinned. No exception is found in the Bible for Mary. Furthermore, over 50 times God is declared to be the *Holy One* in the Bible. Never is the *Mary of the Bible* identified this way; neither are we to pray to Mary (nor any saint or angel), but only to the Heavenly Father and the Lord Jesus, according to God's Word.

2.   There is no shred of evidence in the Bible that Mary was resurrected bodily into Heaven.

3.   According to the Book of Revelation, the Church in Paradise is centered around the Heavenly Father and Jesus (Rev. 4:2–5:10), with no mention of Mary, even in the slightest way.

4.   There is no shred of evidence in the Bible that Mary was the cause of her own salvation nor the whole human race. In no salvation message, that is recorded in the Bible, is Mary mentioned by name or even implied!

5.   There is no shred of evidence in the Bible that Mary was redeemed at the point of her conception. All evidence leads one to conclude that she was in no way different from any other person who needs forgiveness and salvation.

6.   There is no shred of evidence in the Bible that Mary is the *ark of the covenant.*

7.   There is no shred of evidence in the Bible that Mary's name, when improperly used, is a violation of the Second Commandment. (In fact, it is really the Third Commandment that forbids the misuse of God's name. The Second Commandment **forbids the making of and bowing before images**. See Ex. 20:4-7.) To include Mary, or any other human, as a misuse of God's name is to lower God to a mere human level.

8. The *gospel,* which is the plan of salvation, doesn't mention or include Mary in the slightest way:

   Now, brothers, I want to remind you of the gospel I preached to you, which you received and on which you have taken your stand. By this gospel you are saved, if you hold firmly to the word I preached to you. Otherwise, you have believed in vain. For what I received I passed on to you as of first importance: that Christ died for our sins according to the Scriptures, that he was buried, that he was raised on the third day according to the Scriptures (1 Cor. 15:1–4).

9. In the Bible, the *Advocate* and *Mediator* is Jesus (1 John 2:1; 1 Tim. 2:5) and the *Helper* is the Lord (Heb. 13:6), with no mention of Mary being any of these; neither is she *Benefactress.*

10. All through the New Testament Jesus is called *life* (Jn. 14:6; 8:12; 6:35; 1 John 5:12; etc.) There is no mention in the Bible of Mary being *life.*

11. Without a doubt, Christian worship has nothing to do, even in the slightest way, with *devotion to Mary.* Please see John 4:23,24.

12. There is no mention in the Scriptures of the *Mary of the Bible* being venerated, called Mother of God, Mother of mercies, ever-virgin, Queen of Heaven, the new Eve, the daughter of Zion or co-operating in the Savior's work. (The only *Queen of Heaven* mentioned in the Bible was a pagan, female goddess that the Israelites got in trouble with God over. See Jer. 7:18–20; 44:17–30.)♥

2

Pope John Paul II On Mary

Certainly, one sure way to know the official position of Roman Catholicism on Mary, besides going to *Vatican Council II* and *The Catechism of the Catholic Church,* is to go to the Pope himself. Such can be easily done by examining the book entitled, *Theotókos.*[1] This book is *a catechesis on Mary, Mother of God* by Pope John Paul II[2] and is comprised of *seventy general audience talks on Mary* which were delivered by him from September 1995 to November 1997.[3] Hence, these are up to date as *a catechesis on Mary* and given by their supreme teaching authority. While Catholicism claims the Pope speaks infallibly at times, it still declares him (even when he isn't speaking infallibly) to be the *supreme pastor and teacher of the faithful,* as we would anticipate. **The following papal quotes will be accepted, without question, by hundreds of millions of trusting Catholics. To them this is the absolute truth about Mary**. But how do his teachings compare with the Biblical record?

---

1   Pope John Paul II, *Theotókos*: Woman, Mother, Disciple, A Catechesis on Mary, Mother of God (Boston: Pauline Books & Media, 2000). *Theotókos* means *Mother of God* and wasn't used until the third century by people in Egypt.

2   John Paul II's personal motto is: ***Mary, I'm all yours.***

3   *Theotókos,* p. 11.

24

Did Mary Take Part In
The Sacrifice At Calvary?

Pope John Paul II would have us all believe the following:

When the Son began his mission, Mary remained in Nazareth, even though this separation did not exclude significant contacts such as the one at Cana. **Above all, it did not prevent her from taking part in the sacrifice of Calvary.**[4]

Just as Eve caused death, so Mary, with her "yes," became **"a cause of salvation" for herself and for all mankind.**[5]

Mary is queen not only because she is Mother of God, but also because, associated as the New Eve with the New Adam, **she cooperated in the work of the redemption of the human race.**[6]

On Calvary, **Mary united herself to the sacrifice of her Son and made her own maternal contribution to the work of salvation,** which took the form of labor pains, the birth of the new humanity.[7]

In contrast to the Catholic teaching that Mary had a role in the sacrifice of Calvary, we read in Scripture that it was only by **the blood of Jesus shed on the cross itself** that *redemption* for mankind was purchased. **His blood alone,** with no mention of Mary's so-called *contribution,* brought about salvation:

---

4   Ibid., pp. 18,19.
5   Ibid., p. 26.
6   Ibid., p. 210.
7   Ibid., p. 234.

He [Jesus] did not enter by means of the blood of goats and calves; but he entered the Most Holy Place once for all **by his own blood,** having obtained **eternal redemption.** (Heb 9:12)

For you know that it was not with perishable things such as silver or gold that you were **redeemed** from the empty way of life handed down to you from your forefathers, but **with the precious blood of Christ,** a lamb without blemish or defect. (1 Pet 1:18,19)

For God was pleased to have all his fullness dwell in him, and through **him** to reconcile to himself all things, whether things on earth or things in heaven, by making peace **through his blood, shed on the cross.** (Col 1:19,20)

As clear as all of that is, the Scriptures add to that by stating that *blood* must be shed to bring about forgiveness of sin. No mention of non-bloody sufferings, such as what Mary experienced, can do that:

In fact, the law requires that nearly everything be cleansed with blood, and **without the shedding of blood there is no forgiveness.** (Heb 9:22)

As kind and as loving as it can be stated, there is not even a single inference to Mary in these Scriptures or anywhere else in the entire Bible, which would even by implication suggest that Mary co-operated with Jesus' blood sacrifice to bring about anyone's salvation. To teach otherwise is to downplay Jesus' incomprehensible blood sacrifice for our salvation and strip glory from Him. Remember, the Bible is to be the Christian's sole source for *teaching* and *correcting* (2 Tim. 3:16, 17).

But If Mary Didn't Give Jesus Birth, Then He Couldn't Have Died for Mankind's Salvation, Right?

I remember witnessing to a Roman Catholic who told me, *But if Mary didn't give Jesus birth, then He couldn't have died for mankind's salvation.* **My response was *and without the Roman soldier that actually nailed Jesus to the cross He couldn't have died for mankind's salvation either. So does this mean we must include the Roman soldier too, whoever he was, in the plan of redemption?* The obvious answer is no.** Besides that it could be added that if Judas hadn't betrayed Jesus into the hands of sinful men, He wouldn't have been crucified for our sins either. Dear reader, **it is *only* by the precious blood of Jesus shed on the cross that mankind can have salvation,** according to the New Testament writers. He alone is the Savior and has the name in which salvation is found:

> He is "the stone you builders rejected, which has become the capstone." **Salvation** is found in **no one else,** for there is **no other name** under heaven given to men by which we must be saved. (Acts 4:11, 12)

Is Mary *Sovereign*?

Sometimes in his *seventy general audience talks on Mary,* Pope John Paul II has quoted other authoritative sources, such as Catholic saints and past popes (just like Alphonsus Liguori did in chapter 3). In doing so in a favorable way, he is personally endorsing their statements. Hence, **Pope John Paul II has gone on record teaching that Mary is *sovereign,* as well as stating other Catholic authorities also believed this in the past, even over a thousand years ago:**

The text passes spontaneously from the expression "the Mother of my Lord" to the title, "my Lady," anticipating what St. John Damascene was later to say. He attributed to Mary the title of **"Sovereign"** ....[8]

In his Encyclical *Ad Coeli Reginam* to which the text of *Lumen Gentium* refers, my venerable Predecessor Pius XII indicates Mary's cooperation in the work of redemption, in addition to her motherhood, as the basis for her queenship. The encyclical recalls the liturgical text: "There was St. Mary, Queen of Heaven and **sovereign of the world** ..." (italics theirs)[9]

John Paul II and other Catholic authorities have chosen to use the word *sovereign* **for Mary. This same word is used in the New International Version of the Bible over 300 times and** *only* **attributed to Almighty God.**

Is Mary *All-Knowing* and *Everywhere Present?*

Some of the unique attributes that only God has are His omniscience (all-knowing) and omnipresence (everywhere present). In the Pope's teachings, he has made the following statements that could lead one to think that Mary also has these attributes:

Thus, far from creating distance between her and us, Mary's glorious state brings about a continuous and caring closeness. **She knows everything that happens in our life** and supports us with maternal love in life's trials.[10]

---

8   Ibid., p. 209. John Damascene died in the eighth century.
9   Ibid., p. 210.
10   Ibid., p. 211.

Question: How could Mary, or any creature, *know every-thing* that happens in the lives of a billion Catholics at the same time? It is impossible unless one wrongly believes such a creature is omniscient like God. The Pope went on to imply Mary's omnipresence:

> One can conclude that the assumption favors Mary's full communion not only with Christ, but with each one of us. **She is beside us,** because **her glorious state enables her to follow us in our daily earthly journey.**[11]

What the Pope taught about Mary is what we are told in the Scriptures about the Lord Jesus:

> ... and teaching them to obey everything I have commanded you. And **surely I am with you always,** to the very end of the age. (Mat 28:20)

Is Mary or God our *Refuge*?

The Pope also teaches the *Mary of Catholicism* is our *protection* and *refuge*:

> From earliest times the Blessed Virgin is honored under the title of Mother of God, under whose **protection** the faithful took **refuge** in all their dangers and necessities.[12]

In contrast to the *Mary of Catholicism*, please note the following Scripture:

> But let all who take **refuge** in you be glad; let them ever sing for joy. Spread your **protection** over them, that those who love your name may rejoice in you. (Psa 5:11)

---

11   Ibid., p. 211.
12   Ibid., p. 245.

Again, we see Catholics being taught something about the *Mary of Catholicism* which only belongs to God.

How different the Pope's message is from the inspired message of the Bible, which states repeatedly that **God is our *refuge*** and ***protection.*** Dear reader, please take several minutes and look up the following Scriptures for yourself: 2 Sam. 22:3, 31; Psa. 2:12; 7:1; 9:9; 11:1; 14:6; 16:1; etc. They, and many others, conflict with the Pope's teaching on Mary. Which will you accept as truth?

The Pope went on to teach:

> By her maternal charity, **she cares for the brethren of her Son,** who still journey on earth surrounded by dangers and difficulties, until they are led into the happiness of their true home. Therefore the Blessed Virgin is invoked by the Church under the titles of Advocate, Auxiliatrix, Adjutrix and Mediatrix.[13]

The Pope would also have us believe Mary will *care* for each of us until we finally get to Heaven. Such not only overly exalts Mary, it would also remove all free will and personal responsibility for the follower of Christ, since Mary has the responsibility to get us into heaven and to *care* for us here in this life:

> Through her closeness to the events of our daily history, **Mary sustains us in trials. She encourages us in difficulty,** always pointing out to us the goal of eternal salvation.[14]

> ... Christians look with **trust** to Mary ...[15]

---

13   Ibid., p. 238.
14   Ibid., p. 55. The Bible says the Holy Spirit is our *Comforter* (Jn. 14:26).
15   Ibid., p. 211.

Is Mary our *Eternal Security*?

Though the Catholic church correctly rejects the teaching of eternal security, the following quote might lead one to believe otherwise:

As a mother, Mary defends her children and **protects them from the harm caused by their own sins.**[16]

The Bible reiterates over and over again that **sin will bring forth spiritual death, even for a righteous person (or Christian).** See Gen. 2:17; Ezek. 18:24; 33:13,18; Lk. 15:24,32; Rom. 8:13; James 1:14-16; 5:19,20; etc. **(Sadly, however, there are many non-Catholics that will deny this Biblical fact, which has led to the spiritual destruction of many.)** But now, from the above papal quote a Catholic could get the wrong impression that Mary will somehow *protect* a Catholic from sin's *harm*. Again, dear reader, **this papal message is not only not found anywhere in the Bible, it is contradictory to Scripture. Please make a note of this.**

We are to Pray *to* Mary

Oftentimes, Catholics will deny that they pray *to* the *Mary of Catholicism*, but the following papal quote is clear:

We ceaselessly **pray to** the Blessed Virgin ...[17]

Please remember, Catholicism declares Mary to be *Mediatrix*. Regarding this, Pope John Paul II has instructed:

---

16   Ibid., p. 238.
17   Ibid., p. 260.

What the Mother asks, the Son approves and the Father grants.[18]

... she obtains what she seeks and **it cannot be denied her.**[19]

As implied elsewhere, Jesus is made subservient to the *Mary of Catholicism.* **It is vital to know the Bible reveals a different Mary, who is nothing like the *Mary of Catholicism*:**

For there is one God and **one mediator** between God and men, the **man** Christ Jesus. (1 Tim 2:5)

Summary

It should be painfully clear that the Pope is not sound in Biblical doctrine, even though many non-Catholics speak well of him as though he is. To be more precise, **he is dangerously wrong on subjects related to *salvation* itself**. He would have us *trust* Mary, whom he thinks took part in the sacrifice at Calvary and much more as just shown. **Dear reader, please believe the Biblical record over the Pope's teaching. Precious souls hang in the balance, including your own.**♥

---

18   Ibid., p. 26.
19   Ibid., p. 211.

3

St. Alphonsus Liguori On Mary

Alphonsus **Mary** Liguori is a well-known, respected figure and influential Catholic Bishop of the past. His teachings have been available for over 250 years. **He was declared *Venerable* in 1796, *beatified* in 1816, *canonized* in 1839 and declared a *Doctor of the Church* in 1871 by Pope Pius IX.** As of 1997 there were **only 33 *Doctors of the Church* with Alphonsus being of this elite number.** To be such a *Doctor* means that his teachings, though not considered *ex cathedra,* were **carefully examined and approved by the Pope, the supreme teacher in the Roman Catholic Church.** Hence, his teachings are believed by his Catholic readership, especially since they carry the endorsements of the *Nihil Obstat* and *Imprimatur.* He has also been considered **an *apostle of Mary*,** since he has done much to exalt her as you will soon read.

The following quotes from Alphonsus are from the book entitled, *The Blessed Virgin Mary*,[1] which was taken from his much larger book, *The Glories of Mary,* first written in 1750. On the back cover of the 2000 edition of *The Glories of Mary,* we read:

---

1 St. Alphonsus Liguori, *The Blessed Virgin Mary* (Rockford, IL: Tan Books and Publishers, Inc., 1982). Nihil Obstat, Thomas L. Kinkead, Censor Librorum. Imprimatur, Michael Augustine, Archbishop of New York.

The Glories of Mary, **widely regarded as Saint Alphonsus Liguori's finest masterpiece, has for two and a half
centuries stood as one of the Catholic Church's greatest
expressions of devotion to the Blessed Virgin. Written
as a defense of Our Lady at a time when Jansenistic
writers were ridiculing Marian devotion,** this classic
work combines numerous citations from the Fathers and
Doctors of the Church with Saint Alphonsus's intense personal piety to produce a timeless treasury of teachings,
prayers, and practices.

Hence, what you are about to read is Liguori's so-called
defense of Our Lady against those who were *ridiculing Marian
devotion.* (Part One of *The Glories of Mary* is his phrase-by-
phrase exposition or commentary of the *Salve Regina.*)

A Detailed Explanation of *Salve Regina*

Among the multitudinous roles and titles given to the *Mary
of Catholicism*, **Alphonsus elaborates on how this Mary is *our
life, our sweetness* and *our hope,* as prayed by hundreds of
millions of Catholics when reciting the Rosary (in the *Salve
Regina*).** Alphonsus cites different sources from the Pope himself down to exalted Catholic saints to Doctors in Catholicism
for the following concepts about Mary, which have been believed by countless millions over the centuries. **Please know
that Vatican Council II has not renounced any of these
teachings about Mary's importance. Liguori's teachings regarding Mary continue to be printed and spread throughout
the world at this present time and he continues to carry the
titles *saint* and *doctor*.**

Mary is *our Life*

There are two primary reasons why Mary is *our life*, according to Doctor Alphonsus:

1.   Mary is our life, because *she obtains for us the pardon of our sins.*[2]

2.   Mary is also our Life, because *she obtains for us perseverance.*[3]

From there the following reasonings are presented as support:

> To understand why the holy Church makes us call **Mary our life** we must know, that **as the soul gives life to the body so does divine grace give life to the soul**; for a soul without grace has the name of being alive, but is in truth **dead**, as it was said of one in the Apocalypse, "Thou hast the name of being alive, and thou art dead." **Mary, then, in obtaining this grace for sinners by her intercession, thus restores them to life.**[4]

> See how the Church makes her speak, **applying to her the following words of Proverbs**: "They that in the morning early watch for me shall find me." ... A little further on she says, "He that shall find me **shall find life, and shall have salvation from the Lord**." "Listen," exclaims St. Bonaventure on these words, "**listen, all you who desire the kingdom of God; honor the most blessed Virgin Mary and you will find life and eternal salvation.**"[5]

---

2   Ibid., p. 49.
3   Ibid., p. 56.
4   Ibid., p .49.
5   Ibid., pp. 49,50.

Catholicism actually attributes Proverbs 8:17-35 to their Mary. [The truth is this chapter is *wisdom* personified and has nothing to do with Mary.]

Besides incredibly misapplying Proverbs 8 to Mary, Alphonsus also quotes another so-called Catholic *saint* who believed *honoring* Mary is the way to *find life and eternal salvation.* **Just knowing that Mary was not even in existence when Proverbs was written refutes the idea that it was her speaking there**. Regarding *honoring* Mary to *find life and eternal salvation,* the Bible has no hint of this. Furthermore, please notice the following Scripture:

> Therefore the LORD, the God of Israel, declares: "I promised that your house and your father's house would minister before me forever." But now **the LORD declares**: "Far be it from me! **Those who honor me I will honor**, but those who despise me will be disdained." (1 Sam 2:30)

All through the Scriptures we are shown that the emphasis is to be on *honoring* God. One is making a very serious mistake to disregard this truth or to exalt another in God's place. God is a *jealous* God (Ex. 20:5; 34:14), who doesn't share his glory with another (Isa. 42:8).

Through Mary *Alone* Can *We Hope For Remission of Our Sins*

After the aforementioned, Aphonsus quotes other likeminded Catholic *saints*:

> With reason, then, does St. Laurence Justinian call her **"the hope of malefactors," since she alone is the one who obtains them pardon from God**. With reason does St. Bernard call her **"the sinners' ladder,"** since she, the most compassionate **Queen, extending her hand to them,**

draws them from an abyss of sin, and enables them to ascend to God. With reason does an ancient writer call **her "the only hope of sinners," for by her help alone can we hope for remission of our sins.**[6]

Therefore, St. Germanus says, "O Mother of God, thy protection never ceases, **thy intercession is life,** and thy patronage never fails." And in a sermon the same saint says, that **to pronounce the name of Mary with affection is a sign of life in the soul,** or at least that **life will soon return there.**[7]

Mary is a Type of *Noah's Ark* and She *Saves* From *Eternal Death*

Mary is that happy ark, says St. Bernard, **"in which those who take refuge will never suffer the shipwreck of eternal perdition."** At the time of the deluge even brutes were saved in Noe's ark. **Under the mantle of Mary even sinners obtain salvation.** St. Gertrude once saw Mary with her mantle extended, and under it many wild beasts—lions, bears, and tigers—had taken refuge. And she remarked that Mary not only did not reject, but even welcomed and caressed, them with the greatest tenderness. **The saint understood hereby that the most abandoned sinners who have recourse to Mary are not only not rejected, but that they are welcomed and saved by her from eternal death.** Let us, then, enter this ark, **let us take refuge under the mantle of Mary, and she most certainly will not reject us, but will secure our salvation.**[8]

---

6   Ibid., pp. 51,52.
7   Ibid., pp. 52,53.
8   Ibid., p. 54.

Now, if it is true (and I hold it as certain, according to the now generally received opinion)—that **all the graces that God dispenses to men pass through the hands of Mary**, it will be equally true that **it is only through Mary that we can hope for this greatest of all graces—perseverance**. And we shall obtain it more certainly if we always **seek it with confidence through Mary**.[9]

Among other things, you have just read a doctrine of Vatican Council II which states that *Mary is the mediatrix of all graces*. Liguori's *salvation* message through the *Mary of Catholicism* continues:

If Mary Condemns you, you will be *Lost*

When a soul **loses devotion to Mary** it is immediately enveloped in darkness, and in that darkness of which the Holy Ghost speaks in the Psalms: "Thou hast appointed darkness, and it is night; in it shall all the beasts of the woods go about." When the light of heaven ceases to shine in a soul, all is darkness, and it becomes the haunt of devils and of every sin. **St. Anselm says, that "if any one is disregarded and condemned by Mary, he is necessarily lost,"** and therefore we may with reason exclaim, "Woe to those who are in opposition to this sun!" **Woe to those who despise its light! that is to say, all who despise devotion to Mary.**[10]

It was, then, not without reason that St. Germanus called the most blessed Virgin the breath of Christians; for **as the body cannot live without breathing, so the soul cannot live without having recourse to and recommending it-**

9   Ibid., p. 56.
10   Ibid., p. 58.

self to Mary, by whose means we certainly acquire and preserve the life of divine grace within our souls.[11]

This is exactly what we should do whenever we are assaulted by temptation: we should not stay to reason with it, but **immediately fly and place ourselves under the mantle of Mary.**[12]

If Mary undertakes our defence we are certain of gaining the kingdom of heaven. "This do, and thou shalt live."[13]

To Cease To Recommend Yourself to Mary = Being *Lost*

If thy heart is thus far moved, it cannot do otherwise than protect me; and if thou protectest me, what can I fear? No, I fear nothing, **I do not fear my sins**, for thou canst provide a remedy; **I do not fear devils**, for thou art more powerful than the whole of hell; **I do not even fear thy Son,** though justly irritated against me, **for at a word of thine He will be appeased. I only fear lest, in my temptations, and by my own fault, I may cease to recommend myself to thee, and thus be lost.**[14]

Mary is *our Sweetness*

Concisely stated about the *Mary of Catholicism* being our *sweetness,* Aphonsus wrote:

---

11 Ibid., p. 59.
12 Ibid., p. 62.
13 Ibid., p. 63.
14 Ibid., p. 63.

Mary our sweetness; she renders death sweet to her clients.[15]

He goes on to explain:

> In their afflictions, and more particularly in the sorrows of death, the greatest that can be endured in this world, **this good Lady and Mother not only does not abandon her faithful servants, but as during our exile she is our life, so also is she at our last hour our sweetness, by obtaining for us a calm and happy death.** For from the day on which Mary had the privilege and sorrow of being present at the death of Jesus her Son, Who was the head of all the predestined, it became her privilege to assist also at their deaths. And for this reason **the holy Church teaches us to beg this most blessed Virgin to assist us, especially at the moment of death: "Pray for us sinners, now and at the hour of our death!"**[16]

Mary, the All-Sufficient Protector

Ah, how quickly do the rebellious spirits fly from the presence of this Queen! **If at the hour of death we have only the protection of Mary, what need we fear from all our infernal enemies?** David, fearing the horrors of death, encouraged himself **by placing his reliance on the death of the coming Redeemer and on the intercession of the virgin Mother.**[17]

Nowhere in the entire Bible does it say these things about Mary, including that David *encouraged himself* by, in part, relying upon Mary's intercession. Moreover, nowhere in Scripture

---

15   Ibid., p. 64.
16   Ibid., p. 64
17   Ibid., p. 66.

is there even a single verse which exalts Mary's *intercession* above any other righteous person's prayers or that she is the ultimate *protector* to have at death. Please don't be misled. Doctor Liguori continues:

> **St. Vincent Ferrer says, that not only does the most blessed Virgin console and refresh them, but that "she receives the souls of the dying.**" This loving Queen takes them under her mantle, and thus presents them to the Judge, her Son, and most certainly obtains their **salvation.**[18]

> Let us, then, be of good heart, though we be sinners, and feel certain that **Mary will come and assist us at death, and comfort and console us with her presence**, provided only that we **serve her with love** during the remainder of the time that we have to be in this world. **Our Queen, one day addressing St. Matilda, promised that she would assist all her clients at death who, during their lives, had faithfully served her. "I, as a most tender mother, will faithfully be present at the death of all who piously serve me, and will console and protect them.**"[19]

> How great, then, should be our confidence in this Queen, knowing her great power with God, and that she is so rich and full of mercy that there is no one living on earth who does not partake of her compassion and favor. This was revealed by the blessed Lady herself to St. Bridget, saying, **"I am the Queen of heaven and the Mother of mercy; I am the joy of the just, and the door through which sinners are brought to God.** There is no sinner on earth so accursed as to be deprived of my mercy; for all, if they receive nothing else through my intercession, receive the

---

18   Ibid., p. 68.
19   Ibid., p. 72.

grace of being less tempted by the devils than they would otherwise have been." "No one," she adds, "unless the irrevocable sentence has been pronounced" (that is, the one pronounced on the damned), "is so cast off by God that he will not return to Him, and enjoy His mercy, if he invokes my aid." "I am called by all **the Mother of mercy,** and truly the mercy of my Son towards men has made me thus merciful towards them;" and **she concludes by saying, "And therefore miserable will he be, and miserable will he be in eternity, who, in this life, having it in his power to invoke me, who am so compassionate to all, and so desirous to assist sinners, is miserable enough not to invoke me, and so is damned."** Let us, then, have recourse, and always have **recourse, to this most sweet Queen, if we would be certain of salvation** ....[20]

Please note that the parts related to salvation/damnation allegedly came from an earlier canonized Catholic saint named Bridget, who had visions of Mary. (Much of what Catholicism teaches about Mary, including sacramentals, has come as a result of Mary *visions.* Examples of such sacramentals are the Rosary, Brown Scapular and Miraculous medal.)

Mary our *Hope*

Doctor Liguori summarizes this section of his writings as:

Mary is the hope of all.[21]

But those who hope in Mary, as Mother of God, who is able to obtain graces and **eternal life** for them, are truly blessed and acceptable to the heart of God, Who desires to see that greatest of His creatures honored; for she loved

---

20   Ibid., pp. 16,17.
21   Ibid., p. 76.

and honored Him in this world more than all men and angels put together. And therefore we justly and reasonably call **the Blessed Virgin our hope, trusting, as Cardinal Bellarmine says, "that we shall obtain through her intercession that which we should not obtain by our own unaided prayers."**[22]

"Hail, then, O hope of my soul!" exclaims St. Ephrem, addressing this divine Mother; **"hail, O certain salvation of Christians**; hail, O helper of sinners; hail, fortress of the faithful and **salvation of the world!"**[23]

O **Mary, thou art all-powerful;** for thy divine Son, to honor thee, complies instantly with all thy desires."

St. Gemanus, recognizing in Mary the source of all our good, and that she delivers us from every evil, thus invokes her: "O my **sovereign** Lady, **thou alone art the one whom God has appointed to be my solace here below; thou art the guide of my pilgrimage, the strength of my weakness, the riches of my poverty, the remedy for the healing of my wounds, the soother of my pains, the end of my captivity, the hope of my salvation!** Hear my prayers, have pity on my tears, I conjure thee, **O thou who art my queen, my refuge, my love, my help, my hope, and my strength.**[24]

If Jesus Rejects Us, Mary Will *Obtain Forgiveness* For Us

"If my Redeemer rejects me on account of my sins, and drives me from His sacred feet, I will cast myself at those of His beloved Mother Mary, and there I will remain pros-

---

22   Ibid., p. 77.
23   Ibid., p. 78.
24   Ibid., p. 80.

trate **until she has obtained my forgiveness**; for this Mother of mercy knows not, and has never known, how to do otherwise than compassionate the miserable, and comply with the desires of the most destitute who fly to her for succor; and therefore," he says, "**if not by duty, at least by compassion, she will engage her Son to pardon me.**"

"Look down upon us, then," let us exclaim, in the words of Euthymius, "look down upon us, O most compassionate Mother; cast thine eyes of mercy on us, for **we are thy servants, and in thee we have placed all our confidence.**"[25]

Concluding Thoughts About the *Mary of Catholicism*

There are so many errors in the aforementioned quotes from Doctor Liguori, as well as the others whom he quoted, that a Bible-believing Christian is hard pressed to know how to respond to the numerous fallacies stated, except at times to simply state that *this is clearly not the message of Scripture.* In fact, it is not even close. **Catholicism has lethally magnified their Mary to such an elevated place in our lives, including our** *salvation,* **that many have been misled to trust in** *her* **instead of Jesus alone for their salvation, as Jesus himself taught. Jesus and his apostles openly declared that Jesus is** *our life* **(John 14:6; Col. 3:4),** *sweetness* **(Mt. 11:29 cf. Acts 7:59) and** *hope* **(1 Tim.1:1), but Catholicism has replaced the only Savior with his own mother or at other times tries to make Mary** *the way* **we get to Jesus for salvation. Either way, such is unscriptural and therefore spiritually deadly to believe.**

Though some today might try to dismiss Doctor Liguori's teachings as *radical Marian devotion* and *not mainstream Catholicism*, remember **much of what you read was from other**

---

25   Ibid., pp. 82, 83.

Catholic authorities including popes. All Liguori did, **with the help of these authorities,** was to expand upon the meaning of the *Mary of Catholicism* being our *life, sweetness* and *hope,* which all present-day Catholics agree upon as they recite the Rosary. Even though Liguori has adversely influenced millions of people with these teachings for 250 years, he remains a Catholic *saint* and *doctor.* Furthermore, even since Vatican Council II, his materials remain easily accessible. **Again, to the student of the Bible, not only are these statements about Mary recognized as unscriptural, they are** *dangerously inaccurate* **and** *idolatrous.* **Without question, multiple authorities in Catholicism have exalted Mary to having a role in one's** *salvation,* **thus misleading millions of trusting souls. Clearly a wrong message for salvation has been and still is being spread by Catholicism.** While Catholicism speaks of Jesus, it also mixes in Mary and other things for salvation, which changes the message and reduces it to **a counterfeit—one that won't bring the desired results**. True salvation is found only in Jesus, with absolutely no trust and help from Mary. This is the message of the Bible and should also be ours if we are claiming to be a follower of Jesus.♥

4

Excerpts From The Little Office Of The Blessed Virgin Mary

The following list of quotes and prayers to Mary are all from the *Little Office of the Blessed Virgin Mary*[1] (LOOTBVM). These will help reinforce the overall present-day picture Catholicism projects about Mary, which is also found in other Catholic sources. (This book carries the *Nihil Obstat* and the *Imprimatur*.)

> Virgin of virgins,
> I choose you today
> as **my sovereign,** my queen, my empress,
> and I declare myself, as I am in fact,
> your servant and **your slave.**
>
> I invoke your royal name of Mary,
> that is, **sovereign Lady,**
> and **beg of you with all my heart**
> **to admit me into the privileged circle**
> **of your family**
> **as one of your servants,**
> **to do your will as a humble slave and loving child.**

---

1   1988 ed., compiled and edited by John E. Rostelle, O.S.A. Those desiring the *Sabbatine Privilege* are to recite the *Little Office of the Blessed Virgin Mary*. See chapter 11 for an explanation of the *Sabbatine Privilege*.

... During my whole life
rule over me
as **your servant and slave.**
At the hour of my death,
as I hope for
at the end of my loving servitude
among the privileged members of your family,
receive my soul
and escort it
into the presence of God.[2]

Apparently, from the above, there are some Catholics who have given themselves to their *sovereign,* Mary, to be her *slave.* The same also wrongly think they are Mary's *child* and want the *Mary of Catholicism,* their *Heaven's Gate, to receive* their *souls* at the hour of their death:

Holy Mary,
my Queen and **sovereign Lady,**
I give you myself,
trusting in your fidelity and your protection.

I surrender myself entirely
to your motherly tenderness,
my body, **my soul,**
all that I am, all that I possess,
for the whole of this day,
for every moment of my life,
and especially at the hour of my death.

I entrust to you once more
all my hopes, all my consolations,
all my anxieties, all my troubles,

---

2   Ibid., pp. 106-108.

my life, my dying breath,
so that by your prayers and merits,
I may have, in all I do, one only goal,
your good pleasure and the holy will of your Son.[3]

Praise to **Mary, Heaven's Gate,**
Guiding Star of Christians' way,
Mother of our Lord and King,
Light and hope to souls astray[4]

As Bible-defined Christians look to God, Catholics look to the *Mary of Catholicism*. This is reality even though some might refuse to acknowledge it:

My Lady,
my refuge, life, and help,
my armor and my boast,
my hope and my strength,
grant that I may enjoy
the ineffable, inconceivable gifts of your Son,
your God and our God,
in the heavenly kingdom.
For I know surely
that **you have power to do as you will** ...[5]

"Those Who Do Not Believe
This Will Be *Damned"*

The following is from a homily of the priest Simon of Cascia:

---

3   Ibid., pp. 126, 127.
4   Ibid., p. 134.
5   Ibid., p. 135.

We must therefore firmly believe that Christ is true God and true man, the Son of **Mary who was a virgin before, during and after his birth. Those who do not believe this will be damned, unless they are converted to the true faith.**[6]

So believing in *the perpetual virginity of Mary* is essential for *salvation*, according to that Catholic priest and others in a teaching position within Catholicism. Hence, according to this priest, all Christians knowledgeable of the Bible who correctly reject the perpetual virginity of Mary will be *damned*. (Please see chapter 7 for details on Mary's virginity.) [At times Catholicism will contradict itself, which is shown by this quote about *damnation*. Such a contradiction **is proof that error exists** without even going to the Bible.]

Memorare

Remember, most loving Virgin Mary,
never was it heard
that anyone who **turned to you for help
was left unaided.**

Inspired by this confidence,
though burdened by my sins,
I run to your protection
for you are my mother.

Mother of the Word of God,
do not despise my words of pleading
but **be merciful and hear my prayer.**
Amen[7]

---

6   Ibid., pp. 183, 184.
7   Ibid., pp. 186,187.

As **Catholics would pray to Mary** and ask her to *be merciful and hear my prayer*, the Bible shows that King **David prayed to God** the same exact words:

Answer me when I call to you, O my righteous God. Give me relief from my distress; **be merciful to me and hear my prayer** (Psa 4:1).

Under the section of *Prayers To The Blessed Virgin Mary* in LOOTBVM various ones are cited:

Ancient Prayer to the Virgin

We turn to you for **protection,**
holy Mother of God.
Listen to our prayers and **help** us in our needs.
Save us from every danger, glorious and blessed Virgin[8]

Again, **the *Mary of Catholicism* is prayed to and trusted in for protection and help instead of God, as the Bible teaches.**

Mary, Help to Those in Need

Mary is prayed to and trusted in for more than just protection and help, as shown in the following prayer:

Holy Mary,
help those in need,
give strength to the weak,
comfort the sorrowful,
pray for God's people,
assist the clergy,

---

8   Ibid., p. 186.

intercede for religious.
May all who seek your **help** experience your
unfailing **protection.**
Amen[9]

Prayer To Mary

Next we have, in part, the *Prayer to Mary* which was composed by Pope John Paul II for the Marian year.

... **Sustain us,** O Virgin Mary, on our journey of faith and **obtain for us the grace of eternal salvation.** O clement, O loving, O sweet Mother of God and our Mother Mary.[10]

So, according to the supreme teacher in Catholicism, we should pray to Mary to receive grace needed for *eternal salvation.* Hence, again we see that Catholicism believes their Mary has a role in one's *salvation* and in many lesser areas as well. Such is the ongoing theme in Catholicism about Mary:

Through you we drink from the wellsprings of salvation, O Blessed Virgin Mary.[11]

Regina Caeli

This *Regina Caeli* is prayed partly to Mary and partly to God, but even the section prayed to God reads:

God of life,
you have given joy to the world
by the resurrection of your Son, our Lord Jesus Christ.

---

9   Ibid., p. 187.
10   Ibid., p. 188.
11   Ibid., p. 114.

Through the prayers of his mother, the Virgin Mary, bring us to the happiness of eternal life.
We ask this through Christ our Lord.
Amen[12]

Does God really work through Mary to bring us to *eternal life* or is this just another fabrication taught about Mary? Dear reader, your answer to that question, whatever it may be, should remove all passivity about the *Mary of Catholicism.*

Finally, all of these quotes and prayers to Mary are just more undeniable proof that Catholicism has dangerously elevated Mary to a role which uniquely belongs to the Lord. **Not only is this Scripturally unsound, but it is actually opposing the Christianity taught by the Lord and his Apostles.** Such a doctrine about Mary will prove to be eternally destructive for all who have been deceived in this way.♥

---

12   Ibid., pp. 189,190.

5

Some Revealing Catholic Titles, Hymns And Prayers To Mary

Just how important is Mary to many Catholics and Catholicism as a whole? The answer to this important question is reflected especially in **her many titles**, but also in **praise songs, feast days and prayers to her**. The way she is esteemed and honored (and oftentimes much more) is so entrenched throughout Catholicism that **you can't separate her from it and still have Catholicism with its many so-called *saints*, *doctors* and *popes* who *trusted* Mary for their own *salvation* and taught this to others.**

79 Catholic Titles for Mary

According to the Catholic encyclopedia, *The Little Office of the Blessed Virgin Mary* (or Little Office of Our Lady) is a liturgical devotion to the Virgin Mary which has been around since the 8th century. By the 14th century reciting the LOOT BVM was **almost universally practiced and regarded as obligatory on all the clergy.** Today it is recited by Dominicans, Carmelites, Augustinians as well as a large number of Franciscans, Tertiaries and pious Catholic laymen. **In it, under the *Litany of the Blessed Virgin* and *Litany of Loreto*, we have 79 of the hundreds (even thousands) of different titles that have**

been attributed to the *Mary of Catholicism* over the years.[1]
Please read them carefully.

Litany of the Blessed Virgin[2]

Holy Mary,
Holy Mother of God,
Most honored of virgins,
Chosen daughter of the Father,
Mother of Christ,
Glory of the Holy Spirit,
Virgin daughter of Zion,
Virgin poor and humble,
Virgin gentle and obedient,
Handmaid of the Lord,
Mother of the Lord,
Helper of the Redeemed,
Full of grace,
Fountain of beauty,
Model of virtue,
Finest fruit of the redemption,
Perfect disciple of Christ,
Untarnished image of the Church,
Woman transformed,
Woman clothed with the sun,
Woman crowned with stars,
Gentile Lady,
Gracious Lady,
Our Lady,
Joy of Israel,
Splendor of the Church,
Pride of the human race,

---

1   See *Appendix B* for a much longer list of Mary titles.
2   *Little Office of the Blessed Virgin Mary* compiled and edited by John E. Rotelle, pp. 190, 191.

Advocate of grace,
Minister of holiness,
Champion of God's people,
Queen of love,
Queen of mercy,
Queen of peace,
Queen of angels,
Queen of patriarchs and prophets,
Queen of apostles and martyrs,
Queen of confessors and virgins,
Queen of all saints,
Queen conceived without original sin,
Queen assumed into heaven,
Queen of all earth,
Queen of heaven,
Queen of the universe

Litany of Loreto[3]

Mother of the Church,
Mother of Divine grace,
Mother most pure,
Mother of chaste love,
Mother and virgin,
Sinless Mother,
Dearest of Mothers,
Model of motherhood,
Mother of good counsel,
Mother of our Creator,
Mother of our Savior,
Virgin most wise,
Virgin rightly praised,
Virgin rightly renowned,

---

3   Ibid., pp. 191, 192.

Virgin most powerful,
Virgin gentle in mercy,
Faithful Virgin,
Mirror of justice,
Throne of wisdom,
Cause of our joy,
Shrine of the Spirit,
Glory of Israel,
Vessel of selfless devotion,
Mystical rose,
Tower of David,
Tower of ivory,
House of gold,
Ark of the covenant,
Gate of heaven,
Morning star,
Health of the sick,
Refuge of sinners,
Comfort of the troubled,
Help of Christians,
Queen of the rosary,
Queen of peace

The Pope himself comments on the *Litany of Loreto*:

> Popular piety frequently adds a litany to the rosary. The best known is the one used at the shrine of Loreto and is therefore called the Litany of Loreto. With very simple invocations, it **helps us concentrate on Mary's person, in order to grasp the spiritual riches which the Father's love poured out in her.**[4]

---

4   *Theotókos*, pp. 256, 257.

Especially the two titles above which are bolded (*Gate of heaven* and *Refuge of sinners*) suggest that within Catholicism, Mary has a role in one's salvation, which is consistent with other authoritative declarations it has made about her.

Catholicism has also dubbed Mary with the titles of *Glory of Israel, Morning Star* **and** *Help of Christians* **as you just read. Please note the following Scriptures, which state these are all titles for God himself or the Lord Jesus:**

He who is the **Glory of Israel** does not lie or change his mind; for he is not a man, that he should change his mind. (1 Sam 15:29)

I, Jesus, have sent my angel to give you this testimony for the churches. I am the Root and the Offspring of David, and the bright **Morning Star**. (Rev 22:16)

So we say with confidence, "**The Lord is my helper**; I will not be afraid. What can man do to me?" (Heb 13:6)

Besides that, Mary is strangely called *Virgin daughter of Zion*, a term attributed in Scripture to the city of Jerusalem (as is *Daughter of Zion*):

What can I say for you? With what can I compare you, O **Daughter of Jerusalem**? To what can I liken you, that I may comfort you, O **Virgin Daughter of Zion**? Your wound is as deep as the sea. Who can heal you? The visions of your prophets were false and worthless; they did not expose your sin to ward off your captivity. The oracles they gave you were false and misleading. (Lam 2:13,14)

This is the word that the LORD has spoken against him: "The **Virgin Daughter of Zion** despises you and mocks you. The **Daughter of Jerusalem** tosses her head as you flee." (2 Ki 19:21)

Shake off your dust; rise up, sit enthroned, O **Jerusalem**. Free yourself from the chains on your neck, O captive **Daughter of Zion.** (Isa 52:2)

St. Alphonsus M. de' Liguori

One of the best known Catholic saints is Alphonsus M. de' Liguori. (The "M" in his name is for *Mary*.) He gave the Catholic church the following prayer, which carries with it an *indulgence of 3 years*. Please note how *the Mary of Catholicism* is viewed, not only by this canonized Catholic saint, but **also by the Catholic church hierarchy as a whole by their endorsement of a** *3 year indulgence for the faithful who recite this prayer with devotion before an image of the Blessed Virgin Mary.* The *Mary of Catholicism* is graphically portrayed in the following prayer to her centering around *salvation:*

Most holy Virgin Immaculate, my Mother Mary, to thee who art the Mother of my Lord, the Queen of the universe, the advocate, the hope, the refuge of sinners, I who am the most miserable of all sinners, have recourse this day. I venerate thee, great Queen, and I thank thee for the many graces thou hast bestowed upon me even unto this day; in particular **for having delivered me from the hell** which I have so often deserved by my sins. I love thee, most dear Lady; and for the love I bear thee, **I promise to serve thee** willingly for ever and to do what I can to make thee loved by others also. **I place in thee all my hopes for salvation**; accept me as thy servant and shelter me under thy mantle, thou who art the Mother of mercy. And **since thou art so powerful with God, deliver me from all temptations, or at least obtain for me the strength to**

overcome them until death. From thee I implore a true love for Jesus Christ. **Through thee I hope to die a holy death**. My dear Mother, by the love thou bearest to Almighty God, I pray thee to assist me always, but most of all at the last moment of my life. Forsake me not then, until **thou shalt see me safe in heaven, there to bless thee and sing of thy mercies through all eternity. Such is my hope**. Amen.[5]

From that prayer is **a crystal clear teaching which points one, not to the Lord Jesus, but instead to *Mary***. It becomes painfully obvious that the many Catholics who believe (and pray) this way, think:

- Mary is *Queen of the universe, the advocate, the hope, the refuge of sinners;*
- Mary is to be thanked for deliverance from **hell**;
- Mary is to be thanked for bestowing many graces;
- Mary is to be served;
- Mary protects and guards as a *shelter* and *Mother of mercies;*
- **Mary is our entire hope of being saved from hell;**
- **Mary is to be our entire hope of salvation;**
- Mary is asked to deliver us from all our sinful temptations;
- Mary can obtain the strength we need to overcome temptations;
- Mary can assist us through life, but especially at the very end;
- Mary's mercies are mentioned in praise songs to her by those in heaven.

5   St. Alphonsus Liguori, *The Blessed Virgin Mary* (Rockford, Illinois: Tan Books and Publishers, Inc., 1982), p. 4. This book was from his much larger one entitled, *The Glories of Mary.*

Akathistos Hymn

The *Akathistos Hymn* is the title of a hymn in honor of the *Mary of Catholicism*. Within this hymn are various *chants* and sections, which also show **the *Mary of Catholicism* has a role in one's *salvation.***

Fifth Chant

Hail, O **you who saved us from the mire of evil deeds!**

Sixth Chant

Hail, **O Rock who quenched those who thirst for Life!**

Ninth Chant

Hail, **O Ship for those who seek Salvation!**

Tenth Chant

Hail, **O Gateway of Salvation!**

Twelfth Chant

Hail, **O salvation of my soul!**

Kontakion

O Mother worthy of all praise, you who have given birth to the Word, the Holiest of the Holy, accept this present offering, deliver all men from every affliction, and **save from the future punishment those who cry out to you**: "Alleluia!"

The Pope tells how some Catholics have expressed their *love and devotion for Mary*:

> Christian people have also expressed their love for Mary by multiplying expressions of their devotion: hymns, prayers and poetic compositions, simple or sometimes of great quality, imbued with that same love for her whom the crucified one gave us as mother. Some of these, such as the **"Akathistos Hymn"** as the **"Salve Regina,"** have deeply marked the faith life of believers.[6]

This is more clear, undeniable and incontestable proof that Catholicism teaches that their Mary has a role in one's *salvation***, as she is to be prayed to, trusted in, praised in song and venerated through images for all of the aforementioned.**

The *Mary of the Bible* has been grossly misrepresented and changed by Catholicism into a sinless, virgin, queen of the universe, gate of heaven and refuge of sinners, who is to be trusted in for salvation and deliverance from hell. Dear reader, as kindly as it can be written, please know that **this kind of emphasis on Mary is** *idolatrous***, as well as being contradictory and antithetical to the teachings of the Lord Jesus and his apostles. Our faith, trust and hope are to be 100% in Jesus, who is our** *life* **and the only** *way* **to heaven, according to Scripture. He** *alone* **can lead us to Paradise. He is the gate of heaven and refuge of sinners. Salvation hinges on us repenting from our sins and placing a trusting-submitting faith in Jesus with no mention of Mary. Notice how Jesus is magnified in the following Scripture:**

> He who **has the Son has life**; he who **does not have the Son of God does not have life. (1 John 5:12)**

---

6   *Theotókos*, p. 34.

As sincere as you may be, you must turn away from your *idolatry* or you will perish:

> But the cowardly, the unbelieving, the vile, the murderers, the sexually immoral, those who practice magic arts, the **idolaters** and all liars—**their place will be in the fiery lake of burning sulfur**. This is the second death. (Rev 21:8)

Mary is never included *with* Jesus in the Scriptures as having even the slightest role in salvation. That is especially clear as shown by *actual salvation sermons recorded in the Bible*, which were preached by Jesus and his apostles. Please read the four gospels and the entire book of Acts to examine these original salvation sermons for yourself. Act upon that vital message for the sake of your eternal destination.♥

6

Is Mary The Mother Of The Church?

Certainly, one of the most important titles ascribed to Mary by Catholicism is the *Mother of the Church*. The Roman Catholic institution gets this Mary-exalting teaching primarily from the words of Jesus, as He hung from the cross:

> When Jesus therefore saw His mother, and the disciple whom He loved standing nearby, He said to His mother, **"Woman, behold, your son!" Then He said to the disciple, "Behold, your mother!"** And from that hour the disciple took her into his own *household.* (John 19:26,27, NASB).

Mary Was a Widow at the Cross

There is another way to interpret the above passage, which is much more consistent with other Scriptures describing Mary and how the first-century Christians viewed her. Before we look at these other relevant passages, let's examine the context of John 19:26,27. At that point in time, Joseph was dead leaving Mary a widow. This is derived from the last time we ever hear of Joseph, which was in Luke 2 when Jesus was in the temple at the age of 12. **Eighteen years later when Jesus began His min-**

istry, **Joseph is never mentioned again with Mary, which is easily understandable if he had died, as many think.** Instead of Joseph being with Mary (which is what we would expect) during Jesus' earthly teaching ministry, at the cross and in the Upper Room, Mary is frequently cited with only her other children (Mt. 12:46-49; Mk. 3:31-34; Lk. 8:19-21; Jn. 2:12; Acts 1:14) or alone (Jn. 19:26,27).

Mary's Other Children Were
Unbelievers When Jesus Died

Furthermore, Mary's other children, born after Jesus, were all unbelievers before he died on the cross. Scripture says:

> After this, Jesus went around in Galilee, purposely staying away from Judea because the Jews there were waiting to take his life. But when the Jewish Feast of Tabernacles was near, Jesus' brothers said to him, "You ought to leave here and go to Judea, so that your disciples may see the miracles you do. No one who wants to become a public figure acts in secret. Since you are doing these things, show yourself to the world." **For even his own brothers did not believe in him.** (John 7:1-5)

So when Jesus was dying on the cross, Mary was a widow and her other children were not believers at that point. (Soon afterwards that changed.) But at that time, Jesus commissioned John to take Mary into his house and care for her, as he would for his own *mother* in the natural, which would make John like a *son* to Mary. **The wiser and stronger takes care of the weaker and more feeble, so John took care of Mary.** To misuse John 19:26,27 by reading into it that Mary was made *Mother of the church* has lead many to an unscriptural focus on Mary for one's spiritual needs, instead of looking to Jesus as the Bible declares.

Christians Care For *Widows*

Also, remember that taking care of widows is foundational to Christianity:

> But if a **widow** has children or grandchildren, these should learn first of all to put their religion into practice by caring for their own family and so repaying their parents and grandparents, for this is pleasing to God. (1 Tim 5:4)

> Religion that God our Father accepts as pure and faultless is this: to look after orphans and **widows in their distress** and to keep oneself from being polluted by the world. (James 1:27)

Jerusalem is our *Mother*

Let us now consider other Scriptural evidence regarding this subject of Mary being the *Mother* of the Church. First, is this title ever given to her or anyone? **Shockingly, it is found in Gal. 4:26, but not ascribed to Mary:**

> But **the Jerusalem that is above** is free, and **she is our mother.**

Clearly, the Lord's apostle taught the heavenly Jerusalem is the *mother* of the church and not Mary. It should also be mentioned that the last time Mary is mentioned in the epistles is in this same chapter, but she was not named, even in the slightest way, as having any exalted role, as would be expected, if she was then the *mother* of the church. This is how Mary was referred to:

> But when the time had fully come, God sent his Son, **born of a woman,** born under law, (Gal 4:4)

Mary is shown in Galatians 4 to be just *a woman* and nothing more. Had Paul believed Mary was the *Mother of the Church* he had a golden opportunity at Galatians 4 to mention it but didn't!

"Who Has Been a *Mother* to Me"

Furthermore, in his epistle to the Romans, Paul mentioned who had "been a *mother* to him," **but it was not Mary, the mother of Jesus:**

Greet **Rufus**, chosen in the Lord, **and his mother, who has been a mother to me, too.** (Rom 16:13)

Rufus' mother was like a *mother* to Paul and the only *mother* figure he mentions. If Mary was the *mother of the church,* as some read into John 19:26,27, could Paul have stated this without a mention of Mary? Never!

Jesus Never Exalted Mary
Over His Other Disciples

It should also be stressed that the Lord Jesus never exalted Mary above his other disciples. Ponder Jesus' eternal words carefully:

Pointing to his disciples, he said, "Here are my **mother** and my brothers. **For whoever does the will of my Father in heaven is my brother and sister and mother.**" (Mat 12:49,50)

"Who are my **mother** and my brothers?" he asked. Then he looked at those seated in a circle around him and said, **"Here are my mother** and my brothers! **Whoever does**

God's will is my brother and sister and **mother**." (Mark 3:33-35)

Now **Jesus' mother** and brothers came to see him, but they were not able to get near him because of the crowd. Someone told him, "Your mother and brothers are standing outside, wanting to see you." He replied, "**My mother and brothers are those who hear God's word and put it into practice**." (Luke 8:19-21)

Interpret Scripture With Scripture

According to the Lord, all of his disciples are equal to Mary. She is not honored above the church as their *mother,* according to the Lord. Why then should anyone interpret John 19:26,27 in a way that is contradictory to these other related Scriptures? We need to let Scripture interpret Scripture.

One must also wonder why John never exalted Mary, or even mentioned her, in any of his epistles! The same can be said about Peter, whom Catholics were taught was the first pope. Certainly, Peter should have exalted Mary, like so many popes have done throughout the centuries, but he apparently didn't think she had any special role in the various subjects he addressed in his epistles, which included salvation, receiving grace, living holy, our redemption and prayer life.

Besides John and Peter not mentioning Mary by name, the same can be said about Paul. **Paul wrote almost half of the New Testament and on almost every subject related to the Christian life, yet never mentioned Mary by name.** He did, however, mention all of the following people: Phoebe (Rom. 16:1); Priscilla and Aquila (Rom. 16:3); Epenetus (Rom. 16:5); Andronicus and Junias (Rom. 16:7); Ampliatus (Rom. 16:8); Urbanus (Rom. 16:9); Apelles and Aristobulus (Rom. 16:10); Herodion and Narcissus (Rom. 16:11); Tryphena, Tryphosa and

Persis (Rom. 16:12); Rufus (Rom. 16:13); Asyncritus, Phlegon, Hermes, Patrobas, Hermas (Rom. 16:14); Philologus, Julia, Nereus (Rom. 16:15); Timothy, Lucius, Jason and Sosipater (Rom. 16:21); Tertius (Rom. 16:22); Gaius, Erastus and Quartus (Rom. 16:23); Sosthenes (1 Cor. 1:1); Chloe (1 Cor. 1:11); Apollos and Cephas (1 Cor. 1:12); Crispus and Gaius (1 Cor. 1:14); Stephanas (1 Cor. 1:16); Barnabas (1 Cor. 9:6); Stephanas, Fortunatus and Achaicus (1Cor. 16:17); Titus (2 Cor. 7:6); King Aretas (2 Cor. 11:32); James (Gal. 1:19); Barnabas (Gal. 2:1); James, Peter and John (Gal. 2:9); Tychicus (Eph. 6:21); Epaphroditus (Phil. 2:25); Euodia and Syntyche (Phil. 4:2); Epaphras (Col. 1:7); Tychicus (Col. 4:7); Onesimus (Col. 4:9); Aristarchus and Mark (Col. 4:10); Justus (Col. 4:11); Luke (Col. 4:14); Nympha (Col. 4:15); Archippus (Col. 4:17); Silas and Timothy (1 Thess. 1:1); Hymenaeus and Alexander (1 Tim. 1:20); Pontius Pilate (1 Tim. 6:13); Lois and Eunice (2 Tim. 1:5); Phygelus and Hermogenes (2 Tim. 1:15); Onesiphorus (2 Tim. 1:16); Hymenaeus and Philetus (2 Tim. 2:17); Demas, Crescens and Titus (2 Tim. 4:10); Luke and Mark (2 Tim. 4:11); Tychicus (2 Tim. 4:12); Carpus (2 Tim. 4:13); Alexander (2 Tim. 4:14); Erastus and Trophimus (2 Tim. 4:20); Eubulus, Pudens, Linus and Claudia (2 Tim. 4:21); Artemas and Tychicus (Titus 3:12); Zenas (Titus 3:13); Philemon (Philemon 1); Apphia and Archippus (Philemon 2); Epaphras (Philemon 23); Mark, Aristarchus and Demas (Philemon 24).

Jesus Refuted Her Publicly

Getting back to Jesus, ponder his eternal teaching, when he publicly refuted a woman **who tried to exalt Mary on the basis that she gave birth to Jesus**:

While Jesus was saying these things, one of the women in the crowd raised her voice and said to Him, "**Blessed is the womb that bore You and the breasts at which You**

nursed." But He said, "**On the contrary, blessed are those who hear the word of God and observe it**." (Luke 11:27,28)

It was as though a present-day Catholic, who was trying to over-exalt Mary in Jesus' presence, was there and was openly refuted in public by the Lord. By doing this, Jesus wants all to know *Mary is not special because she bore and helped to raise him.* This fact is a death blow to the *Mary of Catholicism.*♥

Mary In The Upper Room

Another very relevant Scriptural passage needs to be cited, which occurred after Jesus' death on the cross and when the disciples numbering 120, including Mary, were all gathered together:

They all joined together constantly in prayer, along with the women and **Mary the mother of Jesus**, and with his brothers. In those days Peter stood up among the believers (a group numbering about a hundred and twenty) and said, "Brothers, the Scripture had to be fulfilled which the Holy Spirit spoke long ago through the mouth of David concerning Judas, who served as guide for those who arrested Jesus—he was one of our number and shared in this ministry." (With the reward he got for his wickedness, Judas bought a field; there he fell headlong, his body burst open and all his intestines spilled out. Everyone in Jerusalem heard about this, so they called that field in their language Akeldama, that is, Field of Blood.) "For," said Peter, "it is written in the book of Psalms, 'May his place be deserted; let there be no one to dwell in it,' and, 'May another take his place of leadership.' Therefore it is necessary to choose one of the men who have been with us the whole time the

Lord Jesus went in and out among us, beginning from John's baptism to the time when Jesus was taken up from us. For one of these must become a witness with us of his resurrection." So they proposed two men: Joseph called Barsabbas (also known as Justus) and Matthias. Then **they prayed, "Lord**, you know everyone's heart. Show us which of these two you have chosen to take over this apostolic ministry, which Judas left to go where he belongs." Then they cast lots, and the lot fell to Matthias; so he was added to the eleven apostles. (Acts 1:14-26)

Peter and John were present, but again there is **the absence of any kind of special honor that was given to Mary, even though she was supposed to be the *Mother* of the church at this point and allegedly declared such just several weeks before!**

The Disciples Didn't Rely on Mary's *Intercession*

Furthermore, the disciples had an important prayer request, but didn't have Mary present it to God! Apparently, **they also didn't consider her intercession as being more powerful than their own nor did they think she was *mediatrix of all graces*.** Instead, they prayed directly to God and without going through a real *saint,* such as Abraham, Ezekiel, Daniel, etc.

Similarly, in Acts 15 when the Council at Jerusalem occurred, Mary was not given any special honors, called upon to intercede or sought out for help in any way. **In fact, Mary is not even mentioned as being there!** Apparently, the Apostles didn't think she had any special abilities that could assist at this extremely important council.

Ponder This

Also, please ponder this about the *Mary of Catholicism's* alleged mothership of the church. Prov 1:8,9 read:

> Listen, my son, to your father's instruction and **do not forsake your mother's teaching**. They will be a garland to grace your head and a chain to adorn your neck.

If Mary is the *Mother of the Church,* **why don't we have any words of wisdom from her to guide us? She wrote no New Testament books. Also, why aren't we shown that Mary was** *gently* **caring for the new converts to Christianity, as we would think is fitting for such a role:**

> But we were **gentle** among you, **like a mother caring for her little children**. (1 Thess 2:7)

The point to all this is Mary is never shown by title or inference, in the whole of Scripture, to be the *Mother of the Church,* **as the** *Mary of Catholicism* **has been exalted to.** In fact, there is only Scriptural evidence to deny this Catholic teaching and none to affirm it, since John 19:26,27 has been distorted.

To focus exclusively in on John 19:26,27 to get this teaching is to mislead precious souls away from the truth and into something different than what the Bible declares about this issue, which has lead to the spiritual destruction of people who are trying to reach out to God, but doing it in an unscriptural manner. **Salvation is only found in Jesus. We get to Him by going directly to Him, sincerely and repentfully, but never through Mary.♥**

7 _____

Mary's Virginity

The Bible gives us many ways whereby we can clearly identify the Messiah. One of these ways is called a *sign* and is specifically linked to his miraculous birth. In the Book of Isaiah we read:

> Therefore the Lord himself shall give you a sign; Behold, a **virgin** shall conceive, and bear a son, and shall call his name Immanuel (7:14, KJV).

Along with many other Scriptures, that passage clearly points us to the Lord Jesus, the Anointed One, who was born of a *virgin*. But even among those who agree that Mary was a *virgin*, at that point in time, there arises a controversy, that being: Did she stay a virgin after Jesus was born? Let's go to the Scriptures to find the answer:

> And **Joseph**, having risen from the sleep, did as the messenger of the Lord directed him, and received his wife, and **did not know her till she brought forth her son**—the first-born, and he called his name Jesus (Matt 1:24,25, Young's Literal).

The Greek word translated *know* in that verse is *ginosko*. It is also used at Lk. 1:34, where it carries the same meaning:

And Mary said unto the messenger, "How shall this be, seeing a husband I do not **know**?" (Young's Literal).

Mary couldn't understand how she could possibly give birth without first coming to *know* her husband, that is, having sexual union. This is the meaning here and in Matt. 1:25 of *ginosko*. Such did not happen between Joseph and Mary *till* Jesus was born (Matt. 1:25).

Please note: Had the Holy Spirit wanted to convey the thought that Mary was a perpetual virgin her whole life through, He could have stopped Matt. 1:25 before the words: *till she brought forth her son.* **Then the sentence could have taught Mary was a perpetual virgin by reading:** *Joseph ... did not know her* **or as the NIV would have read:** *But he had no union with her.* **This, however, is not how the Biblical record reads!** That verse states, by implication, that there was a future point in time that Joseph and Mary had sexual union, that is, after Jesus was born. This is in perfect agreement with Isa. 7:14, and the other passages on this topic, yet to be cited in this chapter.

Let's move on to a clear supportive text from Luke's Gospel:

And she gave birth to **her firstborn**, a son. She wrapped him in cloths and placed him in a manger, because there was no room for them in the inn (Luke 2:7).

The word *firstborn* is used elsewhere for **the oldest of the children**. Many examples in Scripture could be cited to prove this. The following are but two:

Joseph named his **firstborn** Manasseh and said, "It is because God has made me forget all my trouble and all my father's household." The second son he named Ephraim and said, "It is because God has made me fruitful in the land of my suffering." (Gen 41:51,52)

The sons of Josiah: Johanan the **firstborn**, Jehoiakim the second son, Zedekiah the third, Shallum the fourth. (1 Chron 3:15)

Jesus was not called Mary's *only-born* but instead Mary's *firstborn*, thereby suggesting Mary had other children, which is indeed the case. A more clear indication of this occurred when Jesus, as a full grown man, came to his hometown (Nazareth) and began to teach. People from there, who apparently knew his family, stated the following in disbelief:

Coming to his hometown, he began teaching the people in their synagogue, and they were amazed. "Where did this man get this wisdom and these miraculous powers?" They asked. "Isn't this the carpenter's son? **Isn't his mother's name Mary, and aren't his brothers James, Joseph, Simon and Judas? Aren't all his sisters with us?** Where then did this man get all these things?" (Matt 13:54-56)

According to that text, Mary had at least four other sons, besides Jesus, and at least two daughters. Some argue that the word *brothers*, found in this passage, merely means relatives such as *cousins*. If that is the true intended meaning, then **one must wonder why the Greek word meaning** *cousin* **(anepsios) was not used there as it was in Col. 4:10:**

My fellow prisoner Aristarchus sends you his greetings, as does Mark, the **cousin** of Barnabas. You have received instructions about him; if he comes to you, welcome him.

Again, in contrast to Col. 4:10, a different Greek word is used in Matt. 13:55—*adelphos.* This Greek word translated *brothers* comes from the word, *delphus,* which means *womb.*

Furthermore, we should also focus our attention in upon the word **sisters** in Matt. 13:56. The Greek word for *sisters* is *adelphe.* It is also found in the following:

> Do not rebuke an older man harshly, but exhort him as if he were your father. Treat younger men as brothers, older women as mothers, and younger women as **sisters**, with absolute purity. (1 Tim 5:1,2)

As in Matt. 13:56, the usage of *adelphe* in 1 Tim. 5:2 means natural sister born as to the same mother. The context from verse 1 shows the meaning to be the natural family. This is how the same Greek word must be understood in Matt. 13:56, since spiritual sister can't fit the context.

Mary had seven or more children: **Jesus the *firstborn*** (or oldest) and at least six others, with at least two or more being daughters. There is even more truth on this subject found in the Old Testament book of Psalms, where it is stated in the first person singular, as being spoken of by Jesus:

"My Own Mother's Sons"

> I am a stranger to my brothers, an alien **to my own mother's sons**; for zeal for your house consumes me, and the insults of those who insult you fall on me. (Psa 69:8,9)

That is a Messianic Psalm, that is, it has application to Messiah Jesus. This is clear since this Psalm is quoted in the New Testament (Jn. 2:17) and shown there to apply to the Lord. The point is: Jesus became *an alien to **my own mother's sons***. This alienation is clearly evident at John 7:3-5. Before we look at that passage, **please note that Scripture explicitly declares** that Jesus' mother had other *sons* (Psalm 69:8)! This verse alone is an irrefutable and devastating blow to the idea that the blessed Mary remained a virgin throughout her lifetime. Remember, Joseph had no sexual union with Mary *till* Jesus, Mary's *firstborn*, came into this world.

In Jn. 7:3-5, we read:

> **Jesus' brothers** said to him, "You ought to leave here and go to Judea, so that your disciples may see the miracles you do. No one who wants to become a public figure acts in secret. Since you are doing these things, show yourself to the world." **For even his own brothers did not believe in him**.

This passage clearly shows the context cannot allow for an interpretation of spiritual *brother*, since the same *did **not** believe in him*! This disbelief in Jesus from his own *brothers*, at that point in time, is shown elsewhere:

> Then Jesus entered a house, and again a crowd gathered, so that he and his disciples were not even able to eat. **When his family heard about this, they went to take charge of him, for they said, "He is out of his mind."** . . . Then **Jesus' mother and brothers** arrived. Standing outside, they sent someone in to call him. A crowd was sitting around him, and they told him, **"Your mother and brothers** are outside looking for you." "Who are my mother and my brothers?" he asked. Then he looked at those seated in a circle around him and said, "Here are my mother and my brothers! Whoever does God's will is my brother and sister and mother." (Mark 3:20,21,31-35)

Yes, you read Scripture right. Even Mary, and her other sons, at one point during Jesus' ministry, thought Jesus was *out of his mind*! This, however, doesn't mean that they didn't afterwards come to believe on Jesus and get filled with the Holy Spirit, for they were in the Upper Room on the day of Pentecost with the other 120:

> They all joined together constantly in prayer, along with the women and **Mary the mother of Jesus, and with his brothers.** (Acts 1:14)

There is additional proof that Jesus' half-brothers came to faith in him. This is shown in 1 Cor. 9:5:

> Don't we have the right to take a believing wife along with us, as do the other apostles and **the Lord's brothers** and Cephas?

There we learn that the Lord's half-brothers were married, as was Cephas (another name for Peter, Jn. 1:42). These husband-wife couples traveled together, as they served God.

Furthermore, regarding Jude and James, who were named in Matt. 13:55 as Jesus' *brothers,* we read the following:

> **Jude**, a servant of Jesus Christ and **a brother of James**. To those who have been called, who are loved by God the Father and kept by Jesus Christ. (Jude 1)

Notice: The writer of the epistle of Jude was also "a brother (adelphos) to James," but most importantly he was a servant of Jesus Christ. So he clearly came to his spiritual senses.

Furthermore, James, the Lord's brother, is mentioned by Paul in Gal. 1:19:

> I saw none of the other apostles—only James, **the Lord's brother.** (Gal. 1:19)

This is an important verse for two reasons: (1) It shows that James not only came to faith in Jesus, but became an apostle. (2) Besides becoming an apostle, he was also *the Lord's brother*. The phrase *the Lord's brother*, used here, can't possibly be limited to mean his spiritual brother, since it is already understood that Jesus' apostles are members of his spiritual family. James was both an apostle and half-brother of Jesus.

So according to Scripture, Mary did not remain a virgin after she gave birth to Jesus. This basic Biblical truth is in direct conflict with what millions of people have been taught, but nonetheless, it is God's truth on this subject. The following is but one quote about Mary's perpetual virginity:

> Mary "remained a virgin in conceiving her Son, a virgin in giving birth to him, a virgin in carrying him, a virgin in nursing him at her breast, **always a virgin.**"[1]

Dear reader, that quote was from the Catholic theologian, Augustine (who also was the original source of modern-day *Calvinism*). The following is another important quote which shows how Roman Catholicism counters Matt. 13:55:

> Against this doctrine the objection is sometimes raised that the Bible mentions brothers and sisters of Jesus. The Church has always understood these passages as not referring to other children of the Virgin Mary. **In fact James and Joseph, "brothers of Jesus," are the sons of another Mary, a disciple of Christ, whom St. Matthew significantly calls "the other Mary." They are close relations of Jesus, according to an Old Testament expression.**[2]

---

1   *Catechism of the Catholic Church*, p. 128.
2   Ibid., p. 126.

Friend, examine Matt. 13:54-56 for yourself, which shows the subjects as being from Jesus' hometown, thereby enabling them to identify His own mother Mary and His natural brothers and sisters. That passage is clear about this:

Coming to **his hometown,** he began teaching the people in their synagogue, and they were amazed. "Where did this man get this wisdom and these miraculous powers?" they asked. **"Isn't this the carpenter's son? Isn't his mother's name Mary**, and aren't his brothers James, Joseph, Simon and Judas? Aren't all his sisters with us? Where then did this man get all these things?"

That passage can't possibly be referring to *the other Mary*, as some want us to believe, but Jesus' own mother!

Moreover, trying to sweep all of the New Testament passages away by stating that the phrase *brothers of Jesus* is merely an *Old Testament expression* is to ignore all the other verses which show **Joseph and the *Mary of the Bible* had sexual union, but not until Jesus was born. Matt. 1:25 couldn't be more clear, especially when considered with Psa. 69:8, which explicitly shows Mary had other children.**

Friend, what you will continue to believe about Mary's perpetual virginity is left entirely up to you. You have read what Scripture declares and what the present-day position from Roman Catholicism declares. But know this, you can't believe both declarations, since they are antithetical to each other. **One must be in error.**

Why Mention Mary's Virginity?

The truth about Mary's virginity is important to know for several reasons:

1. **According to Catholic tradition from Augustine of Hippo, *heretics* deny Mary's perpetual virginity.** Consider what he wrote:

    Heretics called Antidicomarites are those who **contradict the perpetual virginity of Mary** and affirm that after Christ was born she was joined as one with her husband.[3]

    Should we conclude that a Christian, who goes by the Scriptural evidence as commanded by 2 Tim. 3:15-17, is a *heretic*, because he rejects Mary's perpetual virginity? God forbid!

2. Another reason why it is important to know the truth about Mary's virginity is because **the *Mary of Catholicism* is not the *Mary of the Bible*.** In other words, the image of Mary, the mother of Jesus, has been changed by Catholicism into something vastly different than the real. She is presented by such as the sinless virgin, Mother of the Church, Mother of Mercies, Door of Paradise, Our Lady of Fatima, The Virgin of the Poor, Lady of the Roses, Co-redemptrix, Queen of Peace, Our Lady of Guadalupe, Mediatrix of all Graces, Mother of God, Refuge of Sinners, Gate of Heaven, Queen of Heaven and much more, even *our life*.

To Jesus Through Mary

Another common teaching regarding her is: *To Jesus Through Mary.* This pronouncement is more serious than Mary's perpetual virginity, for it is directly related to salvation and can, therefore, affect our eternal destiny.

Let's consider the former, *To Jesus Through Mary.* In other words, must we go through Mary to get to the Savior? To find

---

3   W. A. Jurgens, *The Faith of the Early Fathers* (Collegeville, MN: The Liturgical Press, 1979), Vol. 3, p. 166.

out for sure what the truth is, we must search the Scriptures. If anyone would know, it certainly would be the Lord Jesus. The following is what the Lord Himself taught about us **coming** to Him:

> **Come to me**, all you who are weary and burdened, and I will give you rest. Take my yoke upon you and learn from me, for I am gentle and humble in heart, and you will find rest for your souls. For my yoke is easy and my burden is light. (Matt 11:28-30)

> Yet you refuse to **come to me** to have life. (John 5:40)

> Then Jesus declared, "I am the bread of life. He who **comes to me** will never go hungry, and he who believes in me will never be thirsty." (John 6:35)

> On the last and greatest day of the Feast, Jesus stood and said in a loud voice, "If anyone is thirsty, let him **come to me** and drink." (John 7:37)

Note: To refuse to *come* [go] to Jesus, as He Himself taught in these verses means we cannot have spiritual life! On the other hand, to go directly to Him is to find salvation for our souls. This vital truth is beautifully exemplified when the dying thief, being crucified next to Jesus, went directly to Jesus, without first going through Mary or anyone else, and he found forgiveness and salvation. The exact word for word exchange is as follows:

> Then he said, "Jesus, remember me when you come into your kingdom." Jesus answered him, "I tell you the truth, today you will be with me **in paradise."**

According to John's Gospel account, Mary was at the foot of the cross at this time, yet **the thief didn't go first to her to get to Jesus; neither did Jesus make the repentant thief go through Mary to come to Him! Remember that basic truth about salvation. If we are going to get to Jesus to find salvation it will have to be as the dying thief did, that is, directly without first going to anyone else!** Also, remember that Jesus doesn't change (Heb. 13:8). So, **if it worked for that dying thief, it will also work for us, which is also the exact way Jesus taught us to "come" to Him (Matt. 11:28-30; Jn. 5:40; 6:35; 7:37).** Finally, remember it wasn't until after the repentant thief came directly to Jesus that the Lord promised him *paradise.* Just knowing this vital truth, about getting to Jesus, won't do anyone any good unless he acts upon it.

Jesus' True Spiritual Family

Jesus declared to become part of His spiritual family we must **do the will of the Father** (Matt. 12:47-50). This is further explained in a parallel passage:

He replied, "My mother and brothers are those who **hear God's word and put it into practice.**" (Lk 8:21)

To do *the will* of the Father is the same as putting God's word into *practice*!

Blessed Mary

Finally, as stated earlier in this article, **Mary is certainly** *blessed* **because she gave birth to the Messiah (Lk. 1:42),** but this should not be over-emphasized as a woman once tried to do in Jesus' presence:

As Jesus was saying these things, a woman in the crowd called out, **"Blessed** is the mother who gave you birth and nursed you." He replied, **"Blessed rather** are those who hear the word of God and obey it." (Lk 11:27,28)

Those words of correction were not the words of some Protestant, but the Lord Jesus Himself! What a shock they are to multitudes, not because they are inconsistent with the rest of Scripture, but because of all the faulty teachings that center around a Mary not taught in the Bible. Remember, Jesus was the real Mary's *firstborn* who taught all to *come* directly to Himself **for their soul's salvation. Never throughout the Gospels did Jesus ever make any sinner go through Mary to come to Him. Never! Furthermore, none of the Lord's Apostles, including Peter, ever taught: "Through Mary to Jesus." Why then should we believe it? Moreover, it is Jesus who is "Our Life, Sweetness and Hope." Dear reader, what you do with this information about Jesus will affect you throughout all of eternity! Verify all Scriptural quotations for yourself with your own bible.♥**

8

The Immaculate Conception

The *Immaculate Conception* is a Catholic term that many have heard of, but few are informed about. Wrongly, many think the *immaculate conception* refers to Jesus being born of a virgin. The truth is **this 1854 papal proclamation states that *Mary was immaculately conceived* and *redeemed* in her mother's womb and remained *sinless* her whole life through**:

> Through the centuries the Church has become ever more aware that Mary, "full of grace" through God, was **redeemed from the moment of her conception**. That is what the dogma of the Immaculate Conception confesses, as Pope Pius IX proclaimed in **1854**:
>
> **The most Blessed Virgin Mary was, from the first moment of her conception**, by a singular grace and privilege of almighty God and by virtue of the merits of Jesus Christ, Savior of the human race, **preserved immune from all stain of original sin.**[1]

A different Catholic source states the following:

---

1   *Catechism of the Catholic Church,* pp. 123, 124.

Demands for a definition of the Immaculate Conception had been received at Rome long before Pius IX, but with his accession to the papacy these demands were renewed with vigor because of the Pope's known veneration for the Mother of God. Among the less-well-known facts of his life is the **cure from epilepsy** that John **Mary** Mastai-Ferretti, the future **Pius IX, attributed to the intercession of the Blessed Virgin. He vowed to do everything in his power to advance her cause and make her better known and loved by the people.**[2]

Exemption from original sin carries with it two corollary consequences: From the time of her conception, Mary was also free from all motions of concupiscence, and also (on attaining the use of reason) **free from every personal sin during the whole of her life.**[3]

Immaculate Mary

From all of that sprung the Catholic praise song to Mary, *Immaculate Mary:*

Immaculate Mary, your praises we sing,
you now reign in splendor with Jesus, our king.
Ave, ave, ave Maria. Ave, ave Maria.

In heaven the blessed your glory proclaim,
on earth, we **your children invoke your fair name.**
Ave, ave, ave Maria. Ave, ave Maria!

The information circulated about the *Mary of Catholicism* continues to go further and further from the Scriptures, as shown

---

2   John A. Hardon, *The Catholic Catechism* (Garden City, NJ: Doubleday & Company, Inc., 1975), p. 156.
3   Ibid., p. 158.

in this song. It not only mentions her being *immaculate*, but also states that **she is co-reigning in heaven with Jesus where the ones there proclaim her glory and on earth children of Mary invoke her name.**

The Vision at Lourdes

Soon after the Pope's 1854 proclamation about the immaculate conception of Mary was the vision at Lourdes France:

> **In his [Pope Pius IX] judgment the Virgin Mary herself wished to confirm by some special sign** the definition that the Vicar of her divine Son had pronounced amid the applause of the whole Church. "Four years had not elapsed when, in the French town at the foot of the Pyrenees, the Virgin Mother showed herself to a simple and innocent girl at the grotto of Messabielle and to this same girl, earnestly inquiring the name of her with whose vision she was favored, with eyes raised to heaven and sweetly saying, she replied '**I am the Immaculate Conception.**'" Following the other visions, thousands of people from every country in the world have made pilgrimages to Lourdes, where "**miraculous favors** were granted them, which excited the admiration of all and **confirmed the Catholic religion as the only one given approval by God.**"[4]

It becomes very clear from Lourdes, as well as other Catholic visions, that Catholic doctrine is taught or reinforced by such visions, especially when accompanied by miracles. The problem with this *proof* is twofold:

1.   Not all miracles are from God. Please see chapter 14.

---

4   Ibid., pp. 162, 163.

2. Other religions, which vehemently reject and oppose Catholicism, also claim visions, miracles and signs from God, but those visions contradict the Catholic visions. With these facts, we know that **the messages communicated in visions are not always true, since** *truth can't contradict truth.*

We must be very careful with visions, since the devil can disguise himself in a venomous attempt to deceive people who believe in God, as shown in Scripture:

And no wonder, for **Satan himself masquerades as an angel of light**. (2 Cor 11:14)

For the devil to *masquerade as an angel of light* means that **he can appear as a** *messenger* **of God**. (The word *angel* means *messenger* in the Greek.) Hence, this Scripture shows that it is possible that the devil could appear as the Virgin Mary to deceive. The only way we can know with absolute certainty the truth about any vision, from any religion, is to examine the doctrinal message communicated in it with the Bible.

The Only Sure Guide To God's Truth

The Bible is to be the sole source of doctrine for the Christian (2 Tim. 3:16,17). When this basic fact is recognized various forms of confusion are immediately cleared up. When the truth of Scripture is received one can find the God of the Bible, if he seeks God with all of his heart:

You will seek me and find me **when you seek me with all your heart.** (Jer 29:13)

Regarding the teaching of the immaculate conception of Mary, all it takes to show the fallacy of it is to ponder and believe the following Scriptures:

> For **all have sinned** and fall short of the glory of God. (Rom 3:23)

Therefore, **Mary has sinned, just like you and I have.** Also, the second part of that verse reveals a unique feature of God's glory, namely He has never sinned at any time, since He is God. So Romans 3:23 is a double blow to the *immaculate conception* of Mary belief, **which has absolutely no real support from the Bible.** Catholicism, however, misuses Luke 1:28 to support the *immaculate conception* of their Mary:

> Luke 1:28 which relates Gabriel's greeting to Mary "Hail, full of grace" **is said to be a reference to her immaculate conception.**[5]

Please know that not all Catholic Bibles say *full of grace* there, only some do. One such translation reads:

> And when the angel had come to her, he said, "Hail, **full of grace**, the Lord is with thee. Blessed art thou among women." (Lk 1:28)[6]

If *full of grace* means Mary was conceived without sin and remained sinless throughout her life, **then the same, and even more, can be said of Stephen, who was *full of grace and power*.** Please note what the same Catholic Bible says:

---

5   Walter A. Elwell, *Evangelical Dictionary of Theology* (Grand Rapids, MI: Baker Book House, 1984), p. 550.

6   The Holy Bible Catholic Action Edition (Gastonia, NC: Good Will Publishers, Inc., 1953), p. 67.

Now Stephen, **full of grace and power**, was working great wonders and signs among the people (Acts 6:8).[7]

Also, Stephen died a martyr (Acts 7:59,60) but there is no Scripture that says Mary did. **Stephen at the hour of his death did not call out to Mary or rely upon her. Instead, he prayed to Jesus and *entrusted himself* to Him**:

> While they were stoning him, **Stephen prayed, "Lord Jesus, receive my spirit**." Then he fell on his knees and cried out, **"Lord, do not hold this sin against them**." When he had said this, he fell asleep. (Acts 7:59,60)

Only Jesus was *Sinless*

Besides Rom. 3:23, **other Scriptures speak of only *one* who was without sin—the Lord Jesus—with never any mention of Mary or anyone else:**

> For we do not have a high priest who is unable to sympathize with our weaknesses, but we have **one** who has been tempted in every way, just as we are—**yet was without sin**. (Heb 4:15)

> Such a high priest meets our need—**one** who is holy, blameless, pure, **set apart from sinners**, exalted above the heavens. (Heb 7:26)

According to these verses of Scripture (or the teaching of the earliest Christian church), **Jesus never sinned. He held this honor uniquely alone and never is any person ever cited with him, as just shown. Everyone else has sinned.** All others have been guilty of sin at sometime in their life:

---

7   Ibid.

For God has bound **all men over to disobedience** so that he may have mercy on them all. (Rom 11:32)

If we claim we have not sinned, we make him out to be a liar and his word has no place in our lives. (1 John 1:10)

Certainly, Mary is included in these last two verses, which indicts her like the rest of us as people who have sinned. Hence, we all need a Savior. **Mary knew her own need of this as shown in the following Scripture:**

And my spirit rejoices in **God my Savior.** (Lk 1:47)

The Real Mary's *Sin Offering*

Another relevant passage to this issue is found in the book of Luke, but often overlooked:

. . . Joseph and Mary took him to Jerusalem to present him to the Lord (as it is written in the Law of the Lord, "Every firstborn male is to be consecrated to the Lord"), **and to offer a sacrifice** in keeping with what is said in the Law of the Lord: "a pair of doves or two young pigeons." (Lk 2:22-24)

What kind of *sacrifice* was it that Joseph and Mary offered?

When the days of her purification for a son or daughter are over, she is to bring to the priest at the entrance to the Tent of Meeting a year-old lamb for a burnt offering and a young pigeon or a dove **for a sin offering.** He shall offer them before the LORD to make atonement for her, and then she will be ceremonially clean from her flow of blood. These are the regulations for the woman who gives birth to a boy or a girl. If she cannot afford a lamb, she is to bring two doves or two young pigeons, one for a burnt offering and **the other for a sin offering.** In this way the priest will make atonement for her, and she will be clean. (Lev 12:6-8)

Clearly, neither Joseph nor Mary herself thought she was sinless.

The *Assumption* Of Mary

Error begets more error. Because of the *immaculate conception* declaration, another *Mary of Catholicism* concept was erected:

> **The 1950 action regarding the assumption of Mary is built upon the declaration of "The Immaculate Conception" (Dec. 8, 1854),** which declared Mary free from original sin. Both issue from the concept of Mary as the "Mother of God." Her special state, Pius XII felt, demanded special treatment. If Mary is indeed "full of grace" (cf. Luke 1:28, 44) **the assumption is a logical concomitant.** Like Jesus, she is sinless, preserved from corruption, resurrected, received into heaven, and a recipient of corporeal glory. Thus Mary is crowned Queen of Heaven and assumes the roles of intercessor and mediator.[8]

Pius XII made this a doctrine necessary for *salvation*:

> **The apostolic constitution *Munificentissimus Deus*, promulgated by Pius XII on November 1, 1950, made it a doctrine necessary for salvation,** stating, "The Immaculate Mother of God, the ever-Virgin Mary, having com-

8   *Evangelical Dictionary of Theology*, p. 696.

pleted the course of her earthly life, was assumed body and soul into heavenly glory."[9]

The assumption of Mary is totally without any Scriptural support. Nothing was written about this before the sixth century:

> Finally, Mariologists teach that after her death Mary was assumed bodily into heaven. **No clear reference to the assumption of Mary appears before the sixth century. It was not generally accepted until the thirteenth and was promulgated by Pius XII in 1950.**[10]

The Conclusion From Scripture

From an unscriptural belief about Mary's conception to her alleged bodily assumption into heaven where she was crowned *Queen*, many have been further misled to trust in her instead of God. This God has revealed His truth in the Bible, which leads us to the **Lord Jesus. God alone is the Christian's *refuge*, *hope*, *strength*, etc. Spiritual *life* is only found in Jesus, according to Scripture. He is to be the object of our faith for *salvation*. This is vital truth for many sincere Catholics because *the Mary of Catholicism is not the Mary of the Bible.***

One is surely making the gravest of all mistakes by rejecting God's eternal truth given to mankind in the Bible for anything else, even if it comes through a vision accompanied by miracles. Dear reader, may this not be the case with you. **Remember, nothing can be wrong with going solely by what the Bible declares, which is foundational to the Christian life as well as salvation itself. This is the only safe, sure way to know God's truth.♥**

---

9   Ibid., p. 696.
10   Ibid., p. 686.

9

Is Mary Clothed With The Sun?

Who is the woman described as being *clothed with the sun* in Revelation 12?[1] Two possibilities exist regarding the identity of this mysterious *woman*. They are *Mary* or *Israel*. **Because the Catholic church thinks this woman is Mary, they have pictures and statues of her in glorious splendor standing on the moon with twelve stars on her head as though she is *Queen*. Is that an accurate interpretation of this chapter or a horrible distortion of God's word which has misled people to trust in Mary for their salvation?** Please read Rev. 12 carefully for yourself from beginning to end:

A great and wondrous sign appeared in heaven: a woman clothed with the sun, with the moon under her feet and **a crown of twelve stars on her head.** She was **pregnant** and cried out in pain as she was about to give birth. Then another sign appeared in heaven: an enormous red dragon with seven heads and ten horns and seven crowns on his heads. His tail swept a third of the stars out of the sky and flung them to the earth. The dragon stood in front of the woman who was about to give birth, **so that he might devour her child the moment it was born. She gave**

---

1   The book of Revelation is called *Apocalypse* in some Catholic Bibles.

birth to a son, a male child, who will rule all the nations with an iron scepter. And her child was snatched up to God and to his throne. **The woman fled into the desert** to a place prepared for her by God, where she might be taken care of for 1,260 days. And there was war in heaven. Michael and his angels fought against the dragon, and the dragon and his angels fought back. But he was not strong enough, and they lost their place in heaven. The great dragon was hurled down—that ancient serpent called the devil, or Satan, who leads the whole world astray. He was hurled to the earth, and his angels with him. Then I heard a loud voice in heaven say: "Now have come the salvation and the power and the kingdom of our God, and the authority of his Christ. For the accuser of our brothers, who accuses them before our God day and night, has been hurled down. They overcame him by the blood of the Lamb and by the word of their testimony; they did not love their lives so much as to shrink from death. Therefore rejoice, you heavens and you who dwell in them! But woe to the earth and the sea, because the devil has gone down to you! He is filled with fury, because he knows that his time is short." When the dragon saw that he had been hurled to the earth, **he pursued the woman who had given birth to the male child. The woman was given the two wings of a great eagle, so that she might fly to the place prepared for her in the desert, where she would be taken care of for a time, times and half a time, out of the serpent's reach.** Then from his mouth the serpent spewed water like a river, to overtake the woman and sweep her away with the torrent. But the earth helped the woman by opening its mouth and swallowing the river that the dragon had spewed out of his mouth. Then the dragon was **enraged at the woman and went off to make war against the rest of her offspring —those who obey God's commandments and hold to the testimony of Jesus.** (Rev 12:1-17)

Because of verse 5, we know this woman is associated with Jesus, but in what way? Is it a maternal association with Mary or by *birth* as through ancestry? The only way we will know is by carefully considering the other details found in this same chapter (and elsewhere in Scripture).

Among those details are the mention of a red *dragon* (v.3) who is later identified as the *devil* (v.9). The devil is concerned about the child and wants to kill him immediately after birth. Instead of the devil succeeding, the child is taken up to God and his throne. The devil pursues the woman into the desert after losing his conflict with Michael:

> When the dragon saw that he had been hurled to the earth, **he pursued the woman who had given birth to the male child. The woman was given the two wings of a great eagle, so that she might fly to the place prepared for her in the desert, where she would be taken care of for a time, times and half a time, out of the serpent's reach.** (Rev. 12:13,14)

Does Mary Have Eagle's Wings?

Clearly, the woman is *symbolic* for she is given *eagle wings* to fly out into the desert to be protected from the devil. **Question: When did Mary, the mother of Jesus, sprout wings and *fly* out into the desert for her own protection? If the Catholic church literally interprets Rev. 12:1-5 as to portray Mary in glorious splendor standing on the moon with twelve stars on her head as though she is Queen, then they should also picture her with *two eagle wings* as she is also described as having!** Maybe this is why the Catholic church only refers to the first part of Rev. chapter 12, but not the latter end (verses 13 and 14) which also describes this symbolic *woman.*

On the other hand, if we understand the woman to be symbolic of *Israel,* then we have the nation of Israel fleeing into the desert for 1,260 days to get away from the devil at the end of this age. This would also fit the symbolic interpretation of a crown with twelve stars on her head:

> Then he [Joseph] had another dream, and he told it to his brothers. "Listen," he said, "I had another dream, and this time the **sun** and **moon** and eleven **stars** were bowing down to me." When he told his father as well as his brothers, his father rebuked him and said, "What is this dream you had? Will your mother and I and your brothers actually come and bow down to the ground before you?" (Gen 37:9, 10)

The Meaning of the Twelve Stars

The *twelves stars* are the twelve tribes of Israel. See also Gen. 49:1-28.

But what about the rest of the woman's *offspring—those who obey God's commandments and hold to the testimony of Jesus,* as mentioned in Rev. 12:17? Who are they? If *Israel* is the woman of Rev. 12, then the offspring are true saints described as *those who obey God's commandments and **hold to the testimony of Jesus***. This is possible because Christianity has its roots in Judaism, with the Messiah and the apostles all being Jewish and Christians being the children of the promise, who are regarded as *Abraham's offspring:*

> **If you belong to Christ, then you are Abraham's seed**, and heirs according to the promise. (Gal 3:29)

> I, **Jesus**, have sent my angel to give you this testimony for the churches. I am the Root and **the Offspring of David**, and the bright Morning Star. (Rev 22:16)

... **The people of Israel**. Theirs is the adoption as sons; theirs the divine glory, the covenants, the receiving of the law, the temple worship and the promises. Theirs are the patriarchs, and from them is **traced the human ancestry of Christ**, who is God over all, forever praised! Amen. It is not as though God's word had failed. For not all who are descended from Israel are Israel. Nor because they are his descendants are they all Abraham's children. On the contrary, "It is through Isaac that your offspring will be reckoned." **In other words, it is not the natural children who are God's children, but it is the children of the promise who are regarded as Abraham's offspring**. (Rom 9:4-8)

Also, when we consider the whole of Scripture regarding the woman of Rev. 12:1–17, it is impossible to conclude that the *Mary of the Bible* is this symbolic person.

Besides all this, here is the only time we actually read of a *queen* in the book of Revelation:

Give her as much torture and grief as the glory and luxury she gave herself. In her heart she boasts, "I sit as **queen**; I am not a widow, and I will never mourn." (18:7)

The context of that verse is *Babylon the great*, which gets destroyed in one hour! **Hence, the *Mary of the Bible* is never shown in the Scriptures to be *Queen of heaven*, as exalted by Catholicism.♥**

10 ———————————————

The Rosary

The Rosary prayer is a very important Catholic distinctive and a crucial part of Catholicism itself, which is used to express *love* and *devotion* to Mary, their *Mother* and *Queen.* Without question, the vast majority of Catholics readily know about the Rosary, especially since all local Catholic churches believe in and practice praying (or reciting) it and the month of October is dedicated to the Rosary. The following is what Catholic children are taught about the Rosary:

> **The Rosary is Our Lady's special prayer**. It is not hard to say. On the big beads we say an **Our Father** and on each small bead a **Hail Mary**. Usually we say a **Glory be to the Father** at the end of each ten Hail Mary's, though this is not strictly necessary. At the very end we may say the **Hail Holy Queen**.[1]

Vatican Council II On The Rosary

Present-day Catholicism has officially stated the following about this prayer in the lives of fellow Catholics:

---

1   *St. Joseph Baltimore Catechism*, official revised edition (New York: Catholic Book Publishing Co., 1964), p. 184.

The contemplative life of religious would be incomplete if it were not directed in **filial love towards her who is the Mother of the Church and of consecrated souls. This love for the Virgin will be manifested with the celebration of her feasts and, in particular, with daily prayer in her honour, especially the Rosary.** The daily recitation of the Rosary is a centuries-old tradition for religious, and so it is not out of place to recall the suitability, beauty and efficacy of this prayer, which proposes for our meditation the mysteries of the Lord's life.[2]

While respecting the freedom of the children of God, the Church has always proposed certain practices of piety to the faithful with particular solicitude and insistence. Among these should be mentioned **the recitation of the Rosary**: 'We now desire, as a continuation of the thought of our predecessors, to recommend strongly the recitation of the family Rosary... There is no doubt that ... **the Rosary should be considered as one of the best and most efficacious prayers** in common that the Christian family is invited to recite. We like to think, and sincerely hope, that when the family gathering becomes a time of prayer the **Rosary** is a frequent and favoured manner of praying'. **In this way, authentic devotion to Mary, which finds expression in sincere love and generous imitation of the Blessed Virgin's** interior spiritual attitude, constitutes a special instrument for nourishing loving communion in the family and for developing conjugal and family spirituality. For she who is the Mother of Christ and of the Church is in a special way the Mother of Christian families, of domestic Churches.[3]

---

2   Vatican Council II (Northport, NY: Costello Pub. Co., 1982), Vol. 2, p. 251.
3   Ibid., pp. 865, 866.

To reiterate and capsulize what you just read, Vatican Council II says:

1. **Your contemplative religious life is incomplete without a *love* for Mary, which is especially manifested by celebrating her *feasts* and praying the Rosary.**

2. **Catholics show their *authentic devotion to Mary* by reciting the Rosary which is supposed to be *one of the best and most efficacious prayers*.**

These statements are the *official* position of present-day Catholicism. To believe otherwise is to show yourself uninformed regarding this Catholic prayer and how it is officially viewed from their perspective. **If someone tells you something in contradiction to these things, they are misrepresenting, intentionally or unintentionally, the importance of the Rosary and present-day Catholicism.**

The Hail Holy Queen

Let's now especially focus in upon how the Rosary prayer is ended:

The Rosary is begun and terminated in various ways. In the U.S., it commences with the recitation of an Our Father, three Hail Marys, and a Glory Be to the Father, and ends with the recitation of the **Hail Holy Queen** and the prayer from the Feast of the Rosary.[4]

The following is the *Hail Holy Queen* prayer which is at the end of the Rosary:

---

4   *The New Catholic Encyclopedia*, Vol. 12, 1967, p. 667.

Hail, Holy **Queen**, **Mother of Mercy**, hail, **our life, our sweetness, and our hope**! To thee do we cry, poor banished children of Eve! To thee do we send up our sighs, mourning and weeping in this vale of tears. Turn then, **most gracious advocate**, thine eyes of mercy toward us; and after this, our exile, show us the blessed fruit of thy womb, Jesus. O clement, O loving, O sweet Virgin Mary!

The *Hail Holy Queen* prayer, which proclaims Mary as *our life, sweetness, hope and most gracious advocate*, has an official endorsement from Vatican II. These concepts are declared every time the Rosary is prayed audibly. By calling Mary *our life*, present-day Catholicism is saying through the Rosary, that **their Mary has a role in our salvation.** According to the Bible, this is *another gospel* (Gal. 1:8,9) and if anyone believes statements like these regarding Mary, **they will not get saved or stay saved, even though they are** *sincere.*

We Must Stay Saved

This issue of staying saved, though entirely overlooked by the eternal security so-called *evangelicals*, is just as important as getting *born again*, for without the former the latter will be useless in getting one into the Kingdom. Since we must endure *to the end* to be saved (Matt. 10:22) and hold firmly *to the end* the confidence we had at first to share in Christ (Heb. 3:14), it is crucial for a Catholic who gets Biblically saved to exit from this type of spiritual environment where such doctrine prevails and where other forms of idolatry are also rampant, and to seek out a Bible-preaching church which centers on Christ alone for salvation.

Also regarding the issues of staying saved and doctrine, the Apostle John wrote in 2 John 9:

Anyone who runs ahead and does not continue in the teaching of Christ **does not have God**; whoever continues in the teaching has both the Father and the Son.

Hence, it is clear that continuing in the teaching of Christ is essential to *continue* **to have God! Therefore, to exchange Christ for Mary as our *life*, as taught in the Rosary and openly proclaimed by present-day Catholicism, is spiritually lethal.**

Besides the *Hail Holy Queen* prayer, there are other reasons why the Rosary should be rejected and with it, present-day Catholicism, according to the Bible. After all, how could any true Christian system which also endorses and promotes the Rosary, correctly claim of itself the following?

The Church is catholic: she promotes the fullness of the faith. She bears in herself and **administers the totality of the means of salvation....**The sole Church of Christ which in the Creed we profess to be one, holy, catholic, and apostolic, ... subsists in **the Catholic Church, which is governed by the successor of Peter and by the bishops in communion with him.** Nevertheless, many elements of sanctification and truth are found outside its visible confines.[5]

To quote again the New Catholic Encyclopedia regarding the Rosary, we read the following about its so-called *mysteries*:

The mysteries are divided into three sets of five, namely, the Joyful Mysteries—the **Annunciation of Christ's Incarnation to Mary, her visit to Elizabeth, the birth of Christ, His presentation in the temple**, His being found in the temple; the Sorrowful Mysteries—the agony of

5   *Catechism of the Catholic Church*, p. 230.

Christ in the garden, His scourging, His crowning with thorns, the carrying of the cross, the crucifixion and death of Christ; the Glorious Mysteries—the Resurrection of Christ, His Ascension into heaven, the sending of the Holy Spirit, **the Assumption of Mary into heaven, her corona-tion as Queen of Heaven**.

Please note: *the Assumption of Mary into heaven* and *her coronation as Queen of Heaven* are complete fabrications with-out any Scriptural backing at all. Yet, these together with *the crucifixion and death of Christ* and *the resurrection of Christ* comprise the *epitome of the whole Gospel*, according to pres-ent-day Catholicism. **This is adding to the already perfect Gospel and thereby making it into something else that no longer has its ability to produce salvation. This is just like adding water to gasoline and trying to run your car engine on that admixture.** (Of these *mysteries* approximately half involve Mary!)

The *Epitome of the Whole Gospel?*

The following shows the Catholic view of the Rosary (and the aforementioned mysteries) as being the *epitome of the whole Gospel*:

The liturgical feasts dedicated to the Mother of God and Marian prayer, such as **the rosary, an 'epitome of the whole Gospel,' express this devotion to the Virgin Mary.**[6]

In stark contrast to the Rosary (with its *mysteries*) being the *epitome of the whole Gospel*, the Apostle Paul clearly outlined

---

6   Ibid., p. 253.

an entirely different Gospel, which he preached—the only one that brings true salvation. The following was his *gospel*:

> Now, brothers, I want to remind you of the gospel I preached to you, which you received and on which you have taken your stand. **By this gospel you are saved, if you hold firmly to the word I preached to you. Otherwise, you have believed in vain.** For what I received I passed on to you as of first importance: that Christ died for our sins according to the Scriptures, that he was buried, that he was raised on the third day according to the Scriptures, and that he appeared to Peter, and then to the Twelve. After that, he appeared to more than five hundred of the brothers at the same time, most of whom are still living, though some have fallen asleep. Then he appeared to James, then to all the apostles, and last of all he appeared to me also, as to one abnormally born. (1 Cor 15:1-8)

> I have declared to both Jews and Greeks that they must turn to God in **repentance** and have **faith in our Lord Jesus**. (Acts 20:21)

In view of all this, Rome's Rosary *gospel* is really *another gospel* (Gal. 1:8,9), which has Mary as our *life* and people allegedly getting *born again* at infant baptism. Yet many are saying Catholicism has changed and is a religious system that we can embrace and have Christian unity with. Even well-known contemporary *Protestant* leaders like Billy Graham, Chuck Colson and Pat Robertson carry this type of message. Others like Hank Hanegraaff and Norman Geisler, who have reputations of being apologists, essentially claim the same.

In review, you just read:

1.	How present-day Catholicism places the highest kinds of endorsements on the Rosary prayer.

2.	The Rosary prayer is *the epitome of the Gospel,* according to present-day Catholicism.

The truth is: Among other things, the Rosary is a prayer that exchanges Jesus for Mary by calling her *our life, sweetness, hope and most gracious advocate*, and exalting her to an idolatrous position as *Queen of Heaven*. These facts reveal this prayer as a spiritual snare for all Catholics, even sincere ones, who are trying to draw near to God.

If a person claims to be *born again* and yet prays Mary is his *life,* it would be suggestive of his current need of salvation, even if he was once saved. We must know that it is only Jesus Christ who can save us from Hell. He alone suffered and shed His blood on the cross to obtain full redemption for us. Therefore, He alone is our *life.* It is to Him we must look. It is to Him we must go. This is what brought salvation results in Bible days and it is still doing the same today.

St. Dominic and the Origin of the Rosary

Did the Twelve Apostles and other first-century Christians pray the Rosary? Certainly many Catholics seem to think so. The facts, however, reveal something very different:

> "The Rosary", says the Roman Breviary, "is a certain form of prayer wherein we say fifteen decades or tens of Hail Marys with an Our Father between each ten, while at each of these fifteen decades we recall successively in pious meditation one of the mysteries of our Redemption." The same lesson for the Feast of the Holy Rosary informs us that when the Albigensian heresy was devastating the

country of Toulouse, **St. Dominic earnestly besought the help of Our Lady and was instructed by her, so tradition asserts, to preach the Rosary among the people as an antidote to heresy and sin.** From that time forward this manner of prayer was "most wonderfully published abroad and developed [promulgari augerique coepit] by **St. Dominic whom different Supreme Pontiffs have in various past ages of their apostolic letters declared to be the institutor and author of the same devotion.**"[7]

The next logical question is **who is St. Dominic and when did he live, since he has been declared to be the** *author* **of the Rosary by various popes. This Catholic saint named** *Dominic* **lived from 1170 to 1221 and had a vision of Mary, which exalted the Rosary. Here are some other details:**

> **Apart from the signal defeat of the Albigensian heretics at the battle of Muret in 1213 which legend has attributed to the recitation of the Rosary by St. Dominic,** it is believed that Heaven has on many occasions rewarded the faith of those who had recourse to this devotion in times of special danger.[8]

> It would appear, therefore, that **the devotion of the Rosary, which tradition says was revealed to Saint Dominic,** had come into general use about this time. To this period, too, has been ascribed **the foundation of the Inquisition by Saint Dominic, and his appointment as the first Inquisitor.**[9]

Since Dominic lived from 1170 to 1221 and he is the *author* of the Rosary, then we can conclude that **for nearly 1,000**

---

7   *Catholic Encyclopedia*, Vol. XIII, on-line edition, under the term *The Rosary*.
8   Ibid., Vol. XIII, under the term *Feast of the Holy Rosary*.
9   Ibid., Vol. V, under the term *St. Dominic*.

years the earliest Christians got along perfectly well without this repetitious prayer. (Also, did you notice that the same St. Dominic was also an *inquisitor?*)

St. Dominic's False Prophecy

There are various ways to identify a false prophet, one of which is stated at Acts 10:43. There we learn that the true prophets tell us we get our sins forgiven (get saved) by *believing* on Jesus. **In contrast to this, Dominic would have us believe Mary is the savior of the world and will accomplish such through the Rosary and Scapular:**

> **St. Dominic then uttered a famous prophecy:** "To my Order, the Blessed Virgin will entrust a devotion to be known as the rosary and to your Order, Angelus, she will entrust a devotion to be known as the scapular. **One day, through the rosary and the scapular, she will save the world.**"[10]

Blessed Alan

Another very important person regarding the popularity of the Rosary was a man known among Catholics as *Blessed Alan*, or Alanus de Rupe (1428-1475):

> **He was indefatigable in what he regarded as his special mission, the preaching and re-establishment of the Rosary, which he did with success throughout northern France, Flanders, and the Netherlands.** His vision of the restoration of the devotion of the Rosary is assigned to the year 1460.[11]

---

10 Francis Johnston, *Fatima: The Great Sign* (Rockford, IL: Tan Books and Publishers, Inc., 1980), p. 111.
11 *Catholic Encyclopedia*, under the term *Alanus de Rupe.*

The Fifteen Promises of Mary
To Those Who Faithfully Pray the Rosary

This chapter on the Rosary would be incomplete without citing and commenting on the famous *Fifteen Promises of Mary to Those who Faithfully Pray the Rosary*, **which millions of Catholics know about.** These Fifteen Promises of the Rosary were allegedly given to St. Dominic and Blessed Alan. The *Mary of Catholicism* promises the following:

1. To all those who shall pray my Rosary devoutly, **I promise my special protection and great graces.**

2. Those who shall persevere in the recitation of my Rosary **will receive some special grace.**

3. **The Rosary will be a very powerful armor against hell; it will destroy vice, deliver from sin and dispel heresy.**

4. The rosary will make virtue and good works flourish, and will obtain for souls the most abundant divine mercies. It will draw the hearts of men from the love of the world and its vanities, and will lift them to the desire of eternal things. Oh, that souls would sanctify themselves by this means.

5. **Those who trust themselves to me through the Rosary will not perish.**

6. Whoever recites my Rosary devoutly reflecting on the mysteries, shall never be overwhelmed by misfortune. He will not experience the anger of God nor will he perish by an unprovided death. **The sinner will be converted; the just will persevere in grace and merit eternal life.**

7. **Those truly devoted to my Rosary shall not die without the sacraments of the Church.**

8. Those who are faithful to recite my Rosary shall have during their life and at their death the light of God and the plenitude of His graces and will share in the merits of the blessed.

9. **I will deliver promptly from purgatory souls devoted to my Rosary.**

10. **True children of my Rosary will enjoy great glory in heaven.**

11. What you shall ask through my Rosary you shall obtain.

12. To those who propagate my Rosary I promise aid in all their necessities.

13. I have obtained from my Son that all the members of the Rosary Confraternity shall have as their intercessors, in life and in death, the entire celestial court.

14. **Those who recite my Rosary faithfully are my beloved children, the brothers and sisters of Jesus Christ.**

15. Devotion to my Rosary is **a special sign of predestination.**

Dear Catholic friend, a *promise* is only as good as the person backing it. Since the *Mary of the Bible* is not able to perform the various things promised, then immediately they should be discarded. Furthermore, the Biblical evidence could only force us to conclude that these *promises* were not made by the *Mary of the Bible*. This will become more evident as you read subsequent chapters. For now, please be assured that all of these so-called *promises* are unscriptural and dangerously misleading. Another such promise is what the *Mary of Catholicism* gave at Fatima:

> It is worth remembering that during the first apparition, Our Lady used the word *must* to Francisco, telling him **he *must* pray "many rosaries" if he wished to enter Heaven.**[12]

Born Again Catholics?

We should ask Catholics who claim to be *born again* what Bible verse(s) they base their salvation upon. Ask them if they realize they were not *born again* at infant baptism. We should also specifically mention that the sacraments, good works, church membership and Mary have absolutely no role in our salvation. If a *born again* Catholic disagrees, we should show him from Scripture what true salvation is. **(The Bible is the sole source and final authority to consult regarding the subject of *salvation* and all spiritual matters, 2 Tim. 3:15-17.)** If they reject the clear teaching of Scripture, their testimony should be considered as not genuine. Remember, not everyone who says, *Lord, Lord* will enter the Kingdom!

If one is truly saved, the Holy Spirit, who is the *Spirit of truth* and who is resident within one who is *born again,* will draw him to truth as found in the Bible. If an experience, vision, testimony and/or miracle contradicts the written word of God on any subject, especially salvation, it should immediately be rejected. If we aren't aware of the Bible's message, great spiritual danger and deception exist, even for the true Christian. A true Christian can be fatally deceived. Hence, it is vital for all Christians to go directly to the Bible itself and read it carefully for themselves. Don't just trust another's interpretation.

---

12   *Fatima*, p. 111.

Furthermore, for Catholics who are truly saved to support by their attendance and money, a religious system that points people to Mary and the baby Jesus instead of **to Jesus alone, without his mother,** is for them to share in that *wicked work* (2 Jn. 11)! A Catholic who gets saved should never be told to go back to Catholicism. We should not treat modern-day Catholicism as just another Christian sect, for it isn't. It has a false plan of salvation, which especially includes the *Mary of Catholicism.*

Tears might even be shed by one's family when he announces he won't be going back to the Catholic church. (The same can be said for a Mormon or Jehovah's Witness who gets saved and changes over to truth.) This means families might become *divided,* but Jesus clearly said this would occur and He went on to say **our love for Him must exceed our love for our families or we are *not worthy* of Him:**

Do you think I came to bring peace on earth? No, I tell you, but division. From now on there will be five in one family **divided** against each other, three against two and two against three. They will be **divided**, father against son and son against father, mother against daughter and daughter against mother, mother-in-law against daughter-in-law and daughter-in-law against mother-in-law. (Lk 12:51-53)

Do not suppose that I have come to bring peace to the earth. I did not come to bring peace, but a sword. For I have come to turn a man against his father, a daughter against her mother, a daughter-in-law against her mother-in-law—a man's enemies will be the members of his own household. **Anyone who loves his father or mother more than me is not worthy of me; anyone who loves his son or daughter more than me is not worthy of me; and anyone who does not take his cross and follow me is not worthy of me.** (Mt 10:34-38)

The *Hail Holy King*—a Prayer to Jesus

If you are a Catholic, you might say, "I've never heard of *The Hail Holy King* prayer." It is a Biblical revision of Rome's ending to the Rosary—the Hail Holy Queen:

Hail, Holy King, our Great Shepherd (Heb. 13:20), hail, our life (Col. 3:4), our sweetness (Mt. 11:29) and our hope (1 Tim. 1:1)! To thee do we cry, poor enslaved to sin (Jn. 8:34) children of the devil (1 Jn. 3:10)! **We willingly turn from idols to serve the true and living God** (1 Thess. 1:9). **We turn from our sins and place 100% of our faith in you, Jesus, for our salvation** (Acts 20:21). Turn then, most gracious advocate (1 Jn. 2:1, KJV), thine eyes of mercy towards us and forgive us all our sins. We trust in you **alone** who died on the cross, shed your blood there and were buried but rose again the third day (1 Cor. 15:1-8; Col. 1:20). You **alone** are the only way to the Father (Jn. 14:6), you **alone** have the only name in which salvation is found (Acts 4:12) and you **alone** are the only mediator between God and man (1 Tim. 2:5). **Our eyes are on you alone, as we turn from all sin, to save us from Hell. O clement, O loving, O precious Lord Jesus.**♥

11

The Brown Scapular

Why do Catholics wear the brown scapular?

Before a direct answer is given to this important question, a brief description and some basic information about the scapular would be most appropriate for some people. The brown scapular in my possession measures 1-1/8" by 1-1/2", is made of cloth and has a picture of Mary holding the baby Jesus in her arms. Under this picture are these surprising words:

Whosoever dies wearing this (brown) scapular **shall not suffer eternal fire**. Mary's promise.

This small rectangular patch of cloth is attached to another similar sized patch of cloth by way of two flat cords which enables them to be draped over one's chest and back. The other piece of cloth also has a message on it underneath a picture of Jesus' face:

Cease! The Holy face of Christ protects me.

Along with this brown scapular came a small information sheet about it which carries the *imprimatur* from Thomas M. O'Leary, D.D., July 16, 1941, Bishop of Springfield. In it we read that the aforementioned promise of escaping eternal fire, because one is wearing the brown scapular, was **made by Mary to Saint Simon Stock[1] on July 16, 1251.**

Mary's Promise to St. Simon Stock

For over seven hundred years, **millions of Catholics** all over the world have regarded the brown scapular with esteem and reverence and worn it in token of **Our Lady's celebrated promise to St. Simon Stock on 16 July 1251:**

> **Take this scapular: it shall be a sign of salvation, a protection in danger and a pledge of peace. Whoever dies wearing this garment shall not suffer eternal fire.**

Afterwards, the Catholic saint Alphonsus Liguori stated:

> Just as men take pride in having others wear their livery, so **the Most Holy Mary** is pleased when **Her servants** wear **Her Scapular** as a mark that they have dedicated themselves to **Her service,** and are members of the **Family of the Mother of God.**

Also we read: "Pope Benedict XV granted an indulgence of 500 days [from Purgatory] each time the Scapular is kissed." Furthermore, it is spuriously alleged that:

> This Devotion and Garment can be traced back to The Old Testament, to the great prophet Elias and the remaining faithful living in the caves of Mount Carmel, and is recommended to sincere people of all faiths.

---

[1]   According to the *Catholic Encyclopedia*: he was born in the County of Kent, England, about 1165 and died in the Carmelite monastery at Bordeaux, France, 16 May, 1265.

A summarizing comment is then presented and followed by a prayer to Mary:

Attach then, great importance to your brown Scapular, **it is an assurance of your salvation,** just as to reject Mary's grace is to **invite perdition**.

'O **Queen,** who art the beauty of Carmel and **the mediatrix of all graces,** pray for us' (prayer from The Raccolta may be said on your Rosary Beads).

St. Robert Bellarmine explains the promise as meaning that **"whoever dies wearing the emblem of Mary will receive the grace of final repentance."** (Obviously, to abuse the promise by sinning at will with the intention of dying in the scapular is a grave evil, for God is not mocked. Our Lady is not promising that those dying in mortal sin will be saved; rather that **those dying in the scapular will not die in mortal sin.**)[2]

Very few Catholic people know about Bellarmine's explanation, which wasn't given until 350 years after Simon Stock received that promise. Without question, **millions of sincere Catholics are simply believing the** *Mary of Catholicism's* **promise to Simon Stock.**

Simon Stock

Johannes Grossi wrote his "Viridarium" about 1430, and he relates that **the Mother of God appeared to Simon Stock with the scapular of the order in her hand. This scapular she gave him with the words**: "Hoc erit tibi et cunctis Carmelitis privilegium, in hoc habitu moriens salvabitur"

---

2   *Fatima*, p. 121. Robert Bellarmine was a Catholic theologian and cardinal who lived from 1542–1621.

(This shall be the privilege for you and for all the Carmel-ites, that **anyone dying in this habit shall be saved**).

... At a later date, probably not until the sixteenth century, instead of the scapular of the order the small scapular was given as a token of the scapular brotherhood. Today the brotherhood regards this as its chief privilege, and one it owes to St. Simon Stock, that **anyone who dies wearing the scapular is not eternally lost**. In this way the chief privilege and entire history of the little Carmelite scapular is connected with the name of St. Simon Stock.[3]

The Sabbatine Privilege

The Brown scapular wearer is entitled to a unique *privilege* that other Catholics are not:

Those wearing the scapular become eligible for what is known as the *sabbatine privilege*. This is understood to mean that those wearing the scapular, **reciting daily the Little Office of Our Lady (or the rosary**, in the case of the Blue Army members), and **observing chastity** according to their state in life, will be **released from Purgatory on the first Saturday after death** (or whatever is the equivalent of the first Saturday in the next life). The privilege is believed to have been based on a bull said to have been issued by Pope John XXII on 3 March 1322 **after receiving the favour in a vision of Our Lady** .... From this it seems that **the Church is willing to accept that such souls will be released from Purgatory soon after death, and especially on a Saturday.**[4]

Wearing the brown scapular is a sign of **personal consecration to Mary:**

---

3   *The Catholic Encyclopedia*, Vol. XIII (Robert Appleton Company, 1912).
4   *Fatima*, pp. 122,123.

We signify our consecration to the Immaculate Heart of Mary by enrolment in and **by wearing the brown scapular** of Our Lady of Mount Carmel, **the 700-year-old sign of personal consecration to the Mother of God.**[5]

Our Lady Of Fatima
Holding The Brown Scapular

Again we see from Marian visions an endorsement of something that is totally against the message of the Bible. In this case, it is the Brown Scapular:

Finally, Lucia alone was privileged to see **Our Lady of Mount Carmel holding out the Brown Scapular** to the world, to signify the Glorious mysteries.[6]

After all of these authoritative Catholic claims and promises, now the original question which was stated in the first sentence of this chapter can be more appropriately addressed—*Why do Catholics wear the brown scapular?*

1. **First and foremost, Catholics wear the brown scapular because they think they will escape eternal fire by doing so! This misguided trust, as sincere as it may be, is only possible because Catholicism does not teach the only way to escape Hell fire is a submissive-enduring faith in Jesus alone (Jn. 14:6; Acts 20: 21; Gal. 3:26; Lk. 8:21).** If they only knew Jesus is the only mediator to the Father (1 Tim. 2:5), has the only name in which salvation is found (Acts 4:12), is the gate (Jn. 10:9), our life (Col. 3:4) and hope (1 Tim. 1:1), then they would never trust in wearing a scapular again, even if the message allegedly originated through a vision from Mary and has a pope's endorsement!

5   Ibid., p. 120.
6   Ibid., p. 52.

2. Among other reasons, the Bible was primarily written to inform us about *salvation* (2 Tim. 3:15). Since it clearly does not mention salvation through the wearing of a scapular (or anything else) we should not think the message about the scapular can deliver us from eternal fire! Since this Catholic message originated from a vision in 1251, **we should also immediately be skeptical about it, for now there would be a way of escaping eternal fire that did not exist before July 16, 1251.**

Further, since Mormons, Seventh-Day Adventists and other similar religious groups also claim authoritative visions which likewise contradict the Bible, we can only conclude that it is impossible for God to be the source of all these visions, since they all contradict each other and even more importantly, the Holy Bible! **Logically, there must be another source of visions, since God wouldn't (even couldn't) give out all these conflicting messages!** The Bible confirms this and reveals who the source is that tries to deceive us through visions. Paul wrote:

> ... **Satan himself masquerades as an angel of light** (2 Cor 11:14).

This is a key verse in evaluating visions. The devil wants to deceive us, and attempts to do so under the appearance of a friend (as he approached Eve in the garden of Eden) or a holy messenger from God through a vision, as apparently was the case in 1251!

3. Please note that wearing the scapular is supposed to be an assurance of your salvation. Again, in contrast to this, the eternal, written Word of God declares the following about assurance of salvation:

He who is **having** the Son, hath the life; he who is not having the Son of God—the life he hath not. These things I did write to you who **are believing** in the name of the Son of God, that ye may **know** the life ye have age-during, and that ye may believe in the name of the Son of God. (1 Jn 5:12,13, Young's Literal Translation)

Please note the present-tense in that passage. The only true assurance of salvation, that is offered by God, comes from *having* (present-tense) the Lord Jesus. Verse 13 is also explicit as it reveals that only those who *are believing* in the name of the Son of God have true assurance of salvation! **Please note the exclusive object of our faith must be Jesus.** No such salvation assurance can be found anywhere in God's Word by trusting anyone or anything else, including wearing the scapular! **In fact, for one to trust in wearing the scapular to escape eternal fire shows that he is not trusting in Jesus, which reveals his lost spiritual condition.**

4.   Though it is alleged that the scapular can be traced back to the Old Testament to the days of the prophet Elias, it is impossible to Scripturally substantiate this claim! There is no Biblical evidence for this claim. Furthermore, **kissing an object can only be associated with idolatry,** and never true worship of God, which has never included the use of a graven image of man, woman, etc. in any form (Deut. 5:8–10 cf. Jn. 4:23,24). Therefore, according to Scripture, we have another solid reason to reject wearing of the scapular and devotion to it.

5.   Please note the way Catholicism views Mary, as expressed in the aforementioned prayer—*Queen* and *mediatrix of all graces.* There is nothing in Scripture to back up either of these ultra-exalting descriptions of Mary.

Many Scriptural objections could be cited to counter the teaching that Mary is Queen of Heaven or mediatrix of all graces. Regarding this latter description of Mary, perhaps no refutation can excel the clarity associated with the conversion of the repentant, dying thief. If one would check the gospel accounts of the Lord's infinite, redemptive death for every single person, he would notice that Mary was at the foot of the cross when Jesus was dying. In spite of this, **the dying thief did not go to Mary to get to Jesus, but went directly to Jesus** (Lk. 23:42,43)! Please note that Jesus did not tell this repentant sinner in need of forgiveness to first go to Mary, the so-called "mediatrix of all graces," so that he could afterwards come to Him! In other words, the repentant thief received all the *graces* needed for salvation totally and completely without any help from Mary. **The Scriptural record shows Mary had absolutely no role at all in this man's salvation.**

Dear reader, be assured that the Lord Jesus will likewise receive us as He did the repentant thief, that is, if we, too, go directly to Jesus in a repentant state as this conversion example reveals. Furthermore, other Scriptures command us to follow this procedure (Matt. 11:28; Jn. 5:40; 6:35; 7:37; etc.)! **Finally, if you try to get to Jesus by first going through Mary, you are in disobedience to His directives and you'll never find Him or the salvation He offers!♥**

12

The Fatima Visions

According to the Catholic church, the Virgin Mary appeared at Fatima, Portugal numerous times in 1917 to three little shepherds named Lucia, Francisco and Jacinta. Since the Roman Catholic church has endorsed and fully accepted these visions as being from God and **they have in turn affected hundreds of millions of people over the years by their messages, then these are very important Marian apparitions**. The Bible commands Christians to *test* all things, which includes visions:

> ***Test* everything.** Hold on to the good. (1 Thess 5:21)

How are we to *test* these visions to ascertain the soundness of the *Mary* of Fatima? The Bible is the *test*. **God's written word won't later contradict his own message.** Hence, we read:

> All Scripture is God-breathed and is useful for **teaching, rebuking, correcting and training in righteousness,** so that **the man of God may be thoroughly equipped for every good work.** (2 Tim 3:16,17)

The Message of Fatima

The visions at Fatima consisting of three apparitions of angels and at least six apparitions of Mary, **would have us focus our attention in upon Mary as our refuge, the way to God, protector, etc. Moreover, according to these Catholic visions, amends for sin are to be made to Mary**. Please carefully note the following statements which were communicated by Mary (or Lucia about Mary) at Fatima:

Jesus wishes to make use of you **to make me known and loved. He wants to establish in the world devotion to my Immaculate Heart.**[1]

I will never leave you. My Immaculate Heart will be your refuge and the way that will lead you to God.[2]

In front of the palm of Our Lady's right hand there was a heart encircled with thorns which pierced it. **We understood that it was the Immaculate Heart of Mary, outraged by the sins of Humanity, and that She wanted reparation.**[3]

What I do remember is that **Our Lady said it was necessary for those persons to say the Rosary in order to obtain the graces during the year. And She continued: "Sacrifice yourself for sinners, and say often, especially when you make some sacrifice: 'Oh Jesus, this is for love of You, for the conversion of sinners, and in rep-**

---

1   *Lucia Speaks on The Message of Fatima* (Washington, NJ: Ave Maria Institute, 1968), p. 26.
2   Ibid, p. 26.
3   Ibid., pp. 26,27.

aration for the sins committed against the Immaculate Heart of Mary.' "[4]

You have seen hell where the souls of poor sinners go. **In order to save them, God wishes to establish in the world devotion to my Immaculate Heart. If you do what I tell you, many souls will be saved, there will be peace.**[5]

And then with a sad expression **She said: "Pray, pray very much and make sacrifices for sinners, for many souls go to hell because they have nobody to pray and make sacrifices for them."**[6]

I want to tell you that I wish a chapel to be **erected here in my honour, for I am the Lady of the Rosary**. Continue to say the Rosary every day.[7]

The 1925 Message to Lucia

Then on December 10, 1925 Mary and the child Jesus appeared, according to Lucia. The child Jesus said:

Have pity on the Heart of your Most Holy Mother. It is covered with the thorns with which ungrateful men pierce it at every moment, and there is no one to remove them with an act of reparation. [8]

Then the personage presenting herself as Mary said to Lucia:

---

4   Ibid., p. 29.
5   Ibid., p. 30.
6   Ibid., p. 35.
7   Ibid., p. 40.
8   Ibid., p. 46.

My daughter, look at My Heart surrounded with the thorns with which ungrateful men piece it at every moment by their blasphemies and ingratitude. You at least, try to console me, and say that **I promise to assist at the hour of death with the graces necessary for salvation all those who, on the first Saturday of five consecutive months, go to Confession and receive Holy Communion, recite five decades of the Rosary and keep me company for a quarter of an hour while meditating on the mysteries of the Rosary, with the intention of making reparation to me.**[9]

Is This The Mary of the Bible?

Please ponder the following evidence presented in these seven points:

1. The Rosary is exalted in these visions, but is anti-scriptural in itself. Jesus taught:

    But when you pray, go into your room, close the door and **pray to your Father**, who is unseen. Then your Father, who sees what is done in secret, will reward you. **And when you pray, do not keep on babbling like pagans, for they think they will be heard because of their many words. Do not be like them,** for your Father knows what you need before you ask him. (Mat 6:6-8)

Nowhere in the Bible are we ever told to pray to Mary or repetitiously, as the Fatima visions would have us do. Furthermore the Rosary would have us wrongly think Mary is *our life*.

---

9   Ibid., pp. 46,47.

The Bible declares Jesus is *our Life*:

I am the bread of **life**. (John 6:48)

Jesus said to her, "I am the resurrection and **the life**. He who believes in me will live, even though he dies" (John 11:25)

Jesus answered, "I am the way and the truth and **the life**. No one comes to the Father except through **me**." (John 14:6)

When Christ, who is your **life**, appears, then you also will appear with him in glory. (Col 3:4)

The life appeared; we have seen it and testify to it, and we proclaim to you the eternal life, which was with the Father and has appeared to us. (1 John 1:2)

And this is the testimony: God has given us eternal life, and this **life** is in his Son. (1 John 5:11)

He who has the Son has **life**; he who does not have the Son of God does not have life. (1 John 5:12)

Dear reader, is Jesus your *life* or is Mary? Your answer will affect your eternal destiny.

2. Does Jesus wish to establish *world devotion* to Mary? Please know that such was never the desire or will of the Lord at any time as expressed in the Bible. **Jesus repeatedly pointed people to Himself**, and rightly so since he is the Savior, our Life, only Hope, all in all, etc. He told people to come to him, follow him, obey him, trust on him, believe on him and remain in him. **The Lord never pointed**

anyone to Mary and Himself. It was never a Son/mother team in the Bible. Please remember this and note the following teachings of Jesus Himself:

Come to me, all you who are weary and burdened, and I will give you rest. (Mat 11:28)

The next day Jesus decided to leave for Galilee. Finding Philip, he said to him, "**Follow me**." (John 1:43)

You diligently study the Scriptures because you think that by them you possess eternal life. These are the Scriptures that testify about me, yet **you refuse to come to me to have life**. (John 5:39,40)

Then Jesus declared, "I am the bread of life. **He who comes to me** will never go hungry, and he who **believes in me** will never be thirsty." (John 6:35)

All that the Father gives me **will come to me**, and whoever **comes to me** I will never drive away. (John 6:37)

On the last and greatest day of the Feast, Jesus stood and said in a loud voice, "If anyone is thirsty, **let him come to me** and drink. Whoever **believes in me**, as the Scripture has said, streams of living water will flow from within him." (John 7:37,38)

When Jesus spoke again to the people, he said, "I am the light of the world. **Whoever follows me** will never walk in darkness, but will have the light of life." (John 8:12)

I am the gate; whoever enters through me will be saved. He will come in and go out, and find pasture. (John 10:9)

I am the good shepherd; I know my sheep and my sheep know me (John 10:14)

My sheep listen to my voice; I know them, and **they follow me**. (John 10:27)

Jesus said to her, "**I am the resurrection and the life**. He who believes in me will live, even though he dies; and whoever lives and **believes in me** will never die. Do you believe this?" (John 11:25,26)

Do not let your hearts be troubled. **Trust in God; trust also in me** (John 14:1)

Jesus answered, "**I am the way and the truth and the life**. No one comes to the Father **except through me**" (John 14:6)

If you love me, you will obey what I command (John 14:15)

Whoever has **my commands and obeys them, he is the one who loves me. He who loves me will be loved by my Father**, and I too will love him and show myself to him. (John 14:21)

Jesus replied, "**If anyone loves me, he will obey my teaching. My Father will love him**, and we will come to him and make our home with him. He who does not love me will not obey my teaching. These words you hear are not my own; they belong to the Father who sent me" (John 14:23,24)

Remain in me, and I will remain in you. No branch can bear fruit by itself; it must remain in the vine. **Neither can you bear fruit unless you remain in me.** (John 15:4)

I am the vine; you are the branches. If a man remains in me and I in him, he will bear much fruit; **apart from me you can do nothing** (John 15:5)

If anyone does not remain in me, he is like a branch that is thrown away and withers; such branches are picked up, thrown into the fire and burned. If you remain in me and my words remain in you, ask whatever you wish, and it will be given you. (John 15:6,7)

in regard to sin, because **men do not believe in me;** (John 16:9)

My prayer is not for them alone. I pray also for **those who will believe in me through their message,** (John 17:20)

When they had finished eating, Jesus said to Simon Peter, "Simon son of John, **do you truly love me** more than these?" "Yes, Lord," he said, "you know that I love you." Jesus said, "Feed my lambs." Again Jesus said, "Simon son of John, **do you truly love me?**" He answered, "Yes, Lord, you know that I love you." Jesus said, "Take care of my sheep." The third time he said to him, "Simon son of John, **do you love me?**" Peter was hurt because Jesus asked him the third time, "Do you love me?" He said, "Lord, you know all things; you know that I love you." Jesus said, "Feed my sheep." (John 21:15-17)

We even see the Holy Spirit will bring *glory* to **Jesus:**

He will bring glory to me by taking from what is mine and making it known to you. (John 16:14)

Our devotion, trust, faith, reliance, love, etc. is to be on Jesus with **no mention of Mary**, based on Jesus' teachings as well as his holy apostles. Moreover, Jesus is the one the Holy Spirit will *glorify*.

3.   The *Mary of the Bible* could never say *I will never leave you*, as proclaimed in these visions. (Nor could she be our *refuge* or *the way* that will lead us to God). Please know it is only God who could promise the disciples that he would never leave them, since God is everywhere present:

Be strong and courageous. Do not be afraid or terrified because of them, for the LORD your God goes with you; **he will never leave you** nor forsake you. (Deu 31:6)

The LORD himself goes before you and will be with you; **he will never leave you** nor forsake you. Do not be afraid; do not be discouraged. (Deu 31:8)

No one will be able to stand up against you all the days of your life. As I was with Moses, so I will be with you; **I will never leave** you nor forsake you. (Josh 1:5)

Also, our *refuge* is clearly God and Jesus—and not Mary too:

My God is my rock, in whom I take **refuge**, my shield and the horn of my salvation. He is my stronghold, my refuge and my savior—from violent men you save me. (2 Sam. 22:3)

As for God, his way is perfect; the word of the LORD is flawless. He is a shield for all who take **refuge** in him. (2 Sam 22:31)

Kiss the Son, lest he be angry and you be destroyed in your way, for his wrath can flare up in a moment. Blessed are all who take **refuge in him**. (Psa 2:12)

The LORD is a refuge for the oppressed, a stronghold in times of trouble. (Psa 9:9)

You evildoers frustrate the plans of the poor, but **the LORD is their refuge.** (Psa 14:6)

The LORD is my rock, my fortress and my deliverer; my God is my rock, **in whom I take refuge**. He is my shield and the horn of my salvation, my stronghold. (Psa 18:2)

Most importantly we must know, **for salvation's sake, that Jesus is** *the way* **(or** *road***) to the Father**:

Jesus answered, "I am **the way** and the truth and the life. **No one comes to the Father except through me**." (John 14:6)

To say Mary is *the way* **to God is to say we should trust in her for salvation, which is not only disobedience but spiritually deadly, according to the Bible.**

4.   To say Mary wants *reparation* for sins committed is to say that we are to make amends, satisfaction and restitution to her for sins, which is incredibly unscriptural. **When people sin they don't sin against Mary since she is not here among the living to be sinned against and neither is she**

deity. People either sin against a living person here among us now or against God, according to the Bible:

No one is greater in this house than I am. My master has withheld nothing from me except you, because you are his wife. How then could I do such a wicked thing and **sin against God**?" (Gen 39:9)

Otherwise, they will teach you to follow all the detestable things they do in worshiping their gods, and you will **sin against the LORD your God**. (Deu 20:18)

As for me, far be it from me that I should **sin against the LORD** by failing to pray for you. And I will teach you the way that is good and right. (1 Sam 12:23)

Then he said, "Go out among the men and tell them, 'Each of you bring me your cattle and sheep, and slaughter them here and eat them. **Do not sin against the LORD** by eating meat with blood still in it.'" So everyone brought his ox that night and slaughtered it there. (1 Sam 14:34)

When **they sin against you**—for there is no one who does not sin—and you become angry with them and give them over to the enemy, who takes them captive to his own land, far away or near; (1 Ki 8:46)

In every case that comes before you from your fellow countrymen who live in the cities—whether bloodshed or other concerns of the law, commands, decrees or ordinances—you are to warn them **not to sin against the LORD**; otherwise his wrath will come on you and your brothers. Do this, and you will not sin. (2 Chr 19:10)

I have hidden your word in my heart **that I might not sin against you.** (Psa 119:11)

For if you forgive men **when they sin against you**, your heavenly Father will also forgive you. (Mat 6:14)

When you **sin against your brothers** in this way and wound their weak conscience, you sin against Christ. (1 Cor 8:12)

5. Unlike what the Fatima visions declare, no one can obtain *grace* by praying the Rosary. **If we could, then there is now a means to obtain grace that never existed for the first 1000 years in Christianity, since praying the Rosary began around then or after.** The Bible says God gives grace to the humble (Jam. 4:6; 1 Pet. 5:5).

6. To save souls from Hell God wants the true gospel to be declared so forgiveness of sins can be found. Such never comes by *devotion to Mary's Immaculate Heart*. The true gospel is summed up as **repentance** towards God and **faith in Christ Jesus (Acts 20:21). We prove our repentance by our deeds (Acts 26:20) and must faithfully endure to the end to be saved (Mt. 10:22). This is the message that Jesus wanted his followers to spread throughout the world. Please note that Mary is not included in the message Jesus gave the disciples to spread.**

Not The *Mary of The Bible*

7. The following is a clear example of *a false gospel*, but nonetheless is part of the salvation message at Fatima. Here again is what the *Mary of Catholicism* said:

I promise to assist at the hour of death with the graces necessary for salvation all those who, on the first Saturday of five consecutive months, go to Confession and receive Holy Communion, recite five decades of the Rosary and **keep me company** for a quarter of an hour while meditating on the mysteries of the Rosary, with the intention of **making reparation to me.**[10]

Dear reader, please know that Mary doesn't have the ability or influence to make such a *promise* **to assist in one's salvation,** but even if she did, her directives are not true since they contradict Jesus' teachings. All this talk about going to confession, receiving communion, reciting 5 decades of the Rosary, etc. is all foreign to the Bible. This was never the message of Jesus, Paul, Peter, John, James, etc. **Did God have his salvation message changed or revised for us since Fatima? If He did, then there is now another way to obtain salvation since the Fatima visions, which is impossible. There has only been one true plan of salvation alongside many counterfeits.** The following is most relevant about a false gospel:

.... Evidently some people are throwing you into confusion and are trying to pervert the gospel of Christ. But even if we or an angel from heaven should preach a gospel other than the one we preached to you, **let him be eternally condemned!** As we have already said, so now I say again: If **anybody** is preaching to you a gospel other than what you accepted, **let him be eternally condemned!** (Gal 1:7-9)

All this evidence from comparing (and contrasting) the message of Fatima to the Bible forces one to conclude the personage representing Mary was **not the** *Mary of the Bible*. The *Mary of the Bible* **never had any role in one's salvation, as al-**

---

10   Ibid., p. 47.

ready proven. **Never did any sinner go to Mary to get to Jesus. Never is Mary shown to have more mercy or compassion on sinners than Jesus did, etc.** The message of Fatima draws our attention and trust away from the Lord Jesus and places them upon a creature (Mary). Even though sincere Catholic people may be trying to reach out to God by observing the Fatima message, **we must come to God the way the Lord taught to receive salvation results.**

The Vision of Moses and Elijah

Peter, John and James had a vision of Moses and Elijah in their *glorious splendor:*

> About eight days after Jesus said this, he took Peter, John and James with him and went up onto a mountain to pray. As he was praying, the appearance of his face changed, and **his clothes became as bright as a flash of lightning.** Two men, **Moses and Elijah, appeared in glorious splendor,** talking with Jesus. **They spoke about his departure, which he was about to bring to fulfillment at Jerusalem.** Peter and his companions were very sleepy, but when they became fully awake, they saw his glory and the two men standing with him. As the men were leaving Jesus, Peter said to him, "Master, it is good for us to be here. **Let us put up three shelters—one for you, one for Moses and one for Elijah."** (He did not know what he was saying.) While he was speaking, a cloud appeared and enveloped them, and they were afraid as they entered the cloud. A voice came from the cloud, saying, **"This is my Son, whom I have chosen; listen to him."** When the voice had spoken, they found that Jesus was alone. The disciples kept this to themselves, and told no one at that time what they had seen. (Lk 9:28-36)

Moses and Elijah spoke with Jesus about his *departure*, which would be fulfilled at Jerusalem. (Jesus' *departure* refers to his physical death.) **Please note that no unscriptural statements were uttered by Moses or Elijah. Nothing they declared would cause one to trust in them for anything, including protection, salvation or anything else.** Furthermore, there was a form of correction that needed to be issued as a result of this vision. It was given to Peter who wrongly wanted to exalt these two men to the same level as the Lord by building a shelter for them as he wanted one also built for the Lord. The voice from the cloud (God the Father) rebuked Peter for even the suggestion that these men are on a par with Jesus and declared that we are *listen to* Jesus.

We can learn from that vision and correction issued to Peter. **Again, please know that even though someone would appear in *glorious splendor*, that in itself doesn't mean that the vision could not be misunderstood, as Peter did. Most importantly, Moses and Elijah didn't speak in any unscriptural way.** They merely spoke with the Lord about his *departure*, which was 100% in accord with Scripture.

Is Mary *Blessed* Because
She Gave Birth To Jesus?

Nearly two thousand years ago, a woman tried to publicly exalt Mary on the basis that she gave birth to Jesus in the presence of the Lord Himself and his disciples. This is how the eternal record states it:

> As Jesus was saying these things, a woman in the crowd called out, "Blessed is the mother who gave you birth and nursed you." He replied, **"Blessed rather are those who hear the word of God and obey it."** (Luke 11:27,28)

Did the Lord approve of her praise of Mary? Holy Writ states that the Lord publicly rebuked that Mary-exalting woman for that notion and set the record straight on who is blessed with these words:

Blessed rather are those who hear the word of God and obey it.

Please note that Jesus wants all to know that **any person hearing and obeying God's word is blessed more than Mary on the basis she gave birth to Jesus**. Dear reader do you believe what Jesus taught here? Please read his eternal words again:

As Jesus was saying these things, a woman in the crowd called out, "Blessed is the mother who gave you birth and nursed you." He replied, "**Blessed rather are those who hear the word of God and obey it**." (Luke 11:27,28)

The Solar Miracle and Healings

If the devil is trying to deceive sincere people through these visions, then how should we view the solar miracle and healings that have occurred there? On July 13th, Lucia requested a miracle from Mary *so that everyone will believe that you have appeared to us.* In response, Mary answered:

Continue to come here every month. In October I will tell you who I am and what I want, and **will perform a miracle so that all may believe**.[11]

The *miracle* on October 13, 1917 is described by Lucia in the following words:

---

11   Ibid., p. 29.

... And opening Her hands, She made them reflect on the sun. While She ascended, the reflection from Her person was projected on the sun itself. That is the reason why I cried aloud "Look at the sun."[12]

Besides the solar miracle there have been reported physical healings over the years at Fatima. Undoubtedly, many would view this as surely being the handiwork of God. But the truth is, if we go to Scripture, we learn **there are two sources of such miraculous/healing power—God and the devil.** Please see chapter 14 on this subject.

The Fatima Discrepancies

On May 13, 1917 when the Mary of Fatima started to appear to the three little shepherd children, among other things, she told them:

I came to ask you to **come here** [Cova da Iria] for **six successive months, on the 13th day at the same hour.** Later I will tell you what I want. And I will return here yet a seventh time.[13]

Wrong Time and Place!

The fourth apparition occurred on August 15, 1917 and in a place different from the Cova da Iria called *Valinhos*.[14] A different source shows a four day discrepancy from this account:

On the afternoon of Sunday **19 August,** Lucia, Francisco and his brother John were pasturing the sheep in a rocky

---

12   Ibid., pp. 40, 41.
13   Ibid., p. 22.
14   Ibid., p. 22.

field known as **Valinhos, about a mile from Fatima,** when suddenly they noticed the beginning of the extraordinary atmospheric phenomena that has preceded the visions in the Cova da Iria.[15]

Note: In both quotes it was **not on the 13th of the month** and **not in the place where Mary told the children to be to see the apparition.** Is it possible the all-knowing God was taken by surprise and had to send Mary to a different place on a different day than originally announced?

Penance For *Salvation*— Drinking Pond Water?

As a result of the Fatima message the three children were influenced in the following way behavior-wise:

> The three children undertook **the most severe penance for the salvation of sinners.** They wore **a rope tightly round their waists**; they gave their lunches to the poor, or even to their sheep; they didn't drink during the furnace-like heat of August 1917—an almost unendurable penance as anyone who has stayed in Fatima during that month will appreciate. Later, **Jacinta even wanted to drink water from a pond frequented by cattle.**[16]

Again, from a Biblical point of view the above statements are far from God's truth, especially in the following ways: (1) **Jesus on Calvary's cross was the all-sufficient and final *sacrifice* for sinners.** There is nothing Lucia, Jacinta or any other person, as sincere as he may be, can do to improve upon that one-time-for-all-sin sacrifice. (2) It is impossible that Mary has been sinned against, as suggested, and that *reparation* (satis-

---

15   *Fatima,* p. 45.
16   Ibid., p. 37.

faction) needs to be made to *her*. (3) In October, the Mary of Fatima revealed herself as the *Lady of the Rosary*.[17] This again shows the spiritual force behind these apparitions is not the same as what gave us the Scriptures, since the Lord commands us not to *pray repetitiously* in Mat. 6:7:

> And when you pray, **do not keep on babbling like pagans, for they think they will be heard because of their many words.**

Getting back to Jacinta drinking pond water, there is no way for us to know if that infected water she drank lead to her early death in February 1920 or not. But it is crystal clear that she unscripturally thought her sufferings could help others come to salvation. Regarding Jacinta's operation and comment we read:

> ...had two ribs removed with only a local anesthetic. Despite the atrocious pain, she never complained, but was heard to murmur repeatedly: **"Now you can convert many sinners Jesus for I suffer so much."**[18]

The *Bad Fruit* of Fatima and Other Visions

Sadly, Jacinta trusted in the *Mary of Catholicism* for her salvation, at least in part, because of the visions she saw:

> During this period her [Jacinta] love of God and Our Lady seems to have risen to ecstatic heights. She never tired repeating: "..... **Sweet Heart of Mary, be my salvation!**"[19]

---

17   *Lucia Speaks on the Message of Fatima*, p. 40.
18   *Fatima*, p. 84.
19   Ibid., pp. 82,83.

Only God knows how many others have likewise been misled through Marian visions over the years. As astronomical as that number is, it becomes even larger if one adds the people deceived by the visions that Joseph Smith and Ellen G. White claim to have had that have adversely affected millions of Mormons and Seventh Day Adventists throughout the years.

Fatima: *a Compendium of the Catholic Faith*

The Bishop of Fatima said:

Fatima as a whole is a compendium of the Catholic Faith.[20]

To be more exact, **the Fatima visions confirmed the following doctrines, most of which are distinctively Catholic and *unscriptural*:**

The apparitions of Our Lady in the following year again emphasise [sic] the priority of **penance** and prayer, particularly the devout daily recitation of the gospel prayer of the **rosary** "which contains all the mysteries of our salvation," as Pope Leo XIII pointed out. Also confirmed in Our Lady's appearances were the doctrine of the Holy Trinity, the **Sacrifice of the Mass**, the **authority of the Pope**, the existence of Heaven, **Purgatory** and Hell, of saints and demons that Modernists try to eliminate, the **meaning and value of suffering,** the evil of sin and **the serious obligation of every committed Christian to the work of atonement,** the necessity of interior conversion, the indwelling of God in the souls of the just by grace, the mystery of Christ's redemption, **the unique role of Mary as our Mediatrix with Christ, the importance of devo-**

---

20   Ibid., inside back cover.

tion to the Sacred Hearts of Jesus and Mary, the practice of the virtues and the spiritual and corporal works of
mercy and so on. Even the doctrine of original sin is implied at Fatima, for the Immaculate Heart of Mary, which
Fatima underlines, clearly brings into focus **the Immaculate Conception** which in turn points to the doctrine of
the Fall.[21]

Another False Gospel

**It is crystal clear from the evidence that the *Mary of
Fatima* is not the *Mary of the Bible*. There is only one way to
be saved and the *Mary of the Bible* is not even indirectly
connected in the smallest manner with our salvation, according to the Scriptures.** This Mary has absolutely no role in
our salvation, that is, unless you accept Scripture-contradicting
Marian visions (and other Catholic materials) that would state
she does. But to do that is to dangerously ignore the fact that the
Scriptures (or sacred writings) are *able to give us the wisdom
that leads to salvation* **through faith which is in Christ Jesus:**

> And that from childhood you have known **the sacred writ-
> ings which are able to give you the wisdom that leads to
> salvation through faith which is in Christ Jesus.** (2 Tim.
> 3:15)

**Notice how the Scriptures will cause us to place our
faith in *Jesus* alone for salvation.** Hence, not only do we not
need to go elsewhere for *salvation* directions, but we can also be
assured all other sources (visions, papal decrees, etc.) that would
differ from what the Scriptures declare are not from the same
source that gave us the Bible.

---

21   Ibid., pp. 75,76.

The *Acid Test* For Visions

Again, the real *test* for Fatima is the message itself and how it parallels or contradicts the message of the Bible. It is not if there are miracles or healings, but the message itself. When such is examined, **Fatima is shown to be of a different source than the one who gave us the Bible.** To be more exact, this different source is an enemy trying to lead us away from absolute 100% trust and reliance on Jesus for our salvation, as declared in the Scriptures. Dear reader, please, for your own soul's sake carefully reread this important chapter and **verify all Scripture references for yourself. Don't just trust another to do this for you. Souls are at stake over this issue.**♥

13 ─────────────────────────

Other Marian Apparitions Besides Fatima

Most apparitions (visions) attributed to the Virgin Mary are very important to Catholics. From Popes on down to local Catholic parishioners, **hundreds of millions** have visited such shrines for various reasons, especially to pray there or receive a personal miracle. Such locations are found around the world:

> They are the numerous shrines in different parts of the world, **where it is believed that God bestows special favors on those who come to pray there. Lourdes** in France, **Fatima** in Portugal, **Montserrat** in Spain, **Assisi** in Italy, **St. Anne de Beaupre** in Canada, **the Martyr's Shrine** in the United States and Canada, **Guadalupe** in Mexico, **Knock** in Ireland, **Banneux** in Belgium, **Czestochowa** in Poland, and the holy places in Palestine **are only some of the best known.** Many shrines were reportedly the scene of some apparition, generally of Christ or the Blessed Virgin, and **before approval by Church authorities had to be carefully examined.** As a matter of record, **most purported apparitions are disapproved and therefore the places do not become Catholic**

shrines. In some countries, the shrines become national symbols of the people's faith.[1]

John Paul II comments on pilgrimages to shrines:

Pilgrimages to Marian shrines, which attract large crowds of the faithful throughout the year, are a sign of the Christian people's common sentiment for the Mother of the Lord. Some of these bulwarks of Marian piety are famous, such as **Lourdes, Fatima, Loreto, Pompei, Guadalupe and Czestochowa**. Others are known only at the national or local level. In all of them, the memory of events associated with recourse to Mary conveys the message of her motherly tenderness, opening our hearts to God's grace.

These places of Marian prayer are a wonderful testimony to God's mercy, which reaches man through Mary's intercession. **The miracles of physical healing, spiritual redemption and conversion are the obvious sign that, with Christ and in the Spirit, Mary is continuing her work as helper and mother.**[2]

Shrines are *Carefully Examined*

Please note that before an apparition of Mary (with or without Jesus) becomes a *shrine* it is *carefully examined* and *most purported apparitions are disapproved.* Hence, the apparitions that have been *approved* were also *carefully examined.* This means Catholic church authorities have read the teachings associated with these visions and they have their *approval.* Since these visions are so influential, these teachings are likewise significant. But according to Catholicism, no Catholic is bound, as

---

1 John A. Hardon, *The Catholic Catechism* (Garden City, NY: Doubleday & Company, Inc., 1975), pp. 551,552.
2 *Theotókos*, p. 35.

a matter of dogma, to accept these Marian apparitions. While this is true, it is also true that **since their leaders have endorsed Fatima, Lourdes, etc., their messages will be embraced by the vast majority. To the Catholic these are messages directly from heaven.** What are these messages? Why did they occur? What effect did they have on people? Especially three are best known and accepted:

> Obviously, **La Salette, Lourdes, and Fatima** do not have to be defended on any grounds. Few authorities would refuse them a place among **the greatest apparitions of Our Lady.**[3]

> A quick glance at the places Our Lady appeared reveals two interesting facts: first, with the exception of the Miraculous Medal apparition, **they are in isolated, inaccessible areas; and second, religion in these areas was ignored, laughed at, or fiercely attacked.**[4]

> God of course chooses His own times and places and occasions for the miraculous, but His power shines forth **most frequently where His Mother is honored and venerated.**[5]

Other sources would add to these and show that sometimes children would see the apparitions. These would occur in an *isolated* area where Mary is already "honored and venerated." Such seems to be the prime conditions for a Mary apparition.

---

3   John Delaney, *A Woman Clothed with the Sun* (New York, NY: Image Books Doubleday, 1990), p. 14.

4   Ibid., p. 21.

5   Ibid., p. 115.

The Mary of Lourdes

Bernadette Soubirous, who later became a canonized saint, was the 14 year old girl who saw a number of apparitions which started in 1858. In part, the account goes like this:

I saw at one of the openings of the rock a rosebush, one only, moving as if it were very windy. Almost at the same time there came out of the interior of the grotto a golden-colored cloud, and soon after **a Lady, young and beautiful, exceedingly beautiful, the like of whom I had never seen,** came and placed herself at the entrance of the opening above the rosebush. She looked at me immediately, smiled at me and signed to me to advance, as if she had been my mother. All fear had left me but I seemed to know no longer where I was. I rubbed my eyes, I shut them, I opened them; but the Lady was still there continuing to smile at me and making me understand that I was not mistaken. Without thinking of what I was doing, I took my rosary in my hands and went on my knees. The Lady made a sign of approval with her head **and herself took into her hands a rosary which hung on her right arm.**[6]

The personal description of how Mary was dressed is as follows. Again, the Mary of these visions is a young girl herself:

She has the appearance of **a young girl of sixteen or seventeen.** She is dressed in a white robe, girdled at the waist with a blue ribbon which flows down all around it. A yoke closes it in graceful pleats at the base of the neck; the sleeves are long and tight-fitting. She wears upon her head a veil which is also white; this veil gives just a glimpse of her hair and then falls down at the back below her waist.

6   Ibid., pp. 122,123.

Her feet are bare but covered by the last folds of her robe except at the point where a yellow rose shines upon each of them. **She holds on her right arm a rosary of white beads with a chain of gold** shining like two roses on her feet."[7]

"I Am The Immaculate Conception"

The young beautiful looking Mary of Lourdes was dressed in white and **had Rosary beads with her when she appeared to Bernadette, which influenced this young girl to recite the Rosary**. Much more important than merely reinforcing confidence in the Rosary the apparition at Lourdes is especially known as **a heavenly endorsement of what the Pope had just stated four years before and all because the Mary of Lourdes identified herself as** *The Immaculate Conception:*

> In her own account of what transpired then, Bernadette said that she asked *aquero* several times to have the kindness to say who she was. *Aquero* at first only smiled, but then she opened her hands "in the manner of the Miraculous Medal," clasped them again to her breast, raised her eyes to heaven, and said, **"I am the Immaculate Conception."**[8]

> The second significant message lies in the fact that it was, to a very large degree, due to Bernadette that the doctrine of **Pius IX, proclaimed only four years prior to the apparition,** became widely known among the masses.... **After the pronouncement, made by the Blessed Virgin Herself, in a local dialect, the situation changed; the doctrine of the Immaculate Conception** did become a matter of general discussion, and people in the community

---

7   Ibid., pp. 124, 125.
8   Sandra L. Zimdars-Swartz, *Encountering Mary* (New York, NY: Avon Books, 1991), p. 55.

began—dimly at first, but little by little with increasing clarity—to understand that Our Lady "in the first instant of the conception was, by a singular grace and privilege of Almighty God in view of the merits of Jesus Christ, the Saviour of the human race, **preserved exempt from all stain of original sin. . . . Her soul at the very moment of its creation and infusion into Her body was clothed in sanctifying grace."**[9]

The Mary of Catholicism as shown in these apparitions as *The Immaculate Conception,* never sinned and was always saved, even from the moment of conception! This unscriptural concept was believed before the Lourdes apparition, but was confirmed and reinforced here.

The Healing Waters of Lourdes

Just like all other approved Catholic visions, the one at Lourdes is an exaltation of Mary and a confirmation of Catholic dogma. Moreover, supernatural things have occurred there, including healing. Many tend to think such is conclusive proof that God has endorsed these visions:

Lourdes has become a leading shrine—perhaps the leading shrine—for the halt, the lame, and the blind from all parts of the world. Its efficacy in certain cases cannot be doubted, even by the most skeptical.[10]

At the time of the eighth apparition came the thrice-repeated warning of "**Penitence!**" and, on the following day, she received the order, "Drink from the fountain and bathe in it." Bernadette was puzzled; there had never been a fountain at Massabieille, or any kind of a natural spring.

---

9   *Woman,* p. 141.
10   Ibid., p. 142.

But, getting off her knees, she began to scratch the loose gravel off the ground which encircled her. Presently, she noticed that this was moist, and then that **a little pool was forming and that bubbles were rising from it.** She cupped her hands together and drank; afterward, she washed her face. The next day, the pool was overflowing and water was dripping down over the rock; **the following day, the trickle had become a real stream.** Of course, it was immediately said—and has been said by skeptics ever since—that the spring was there all the time, but that no one had happened to notice it, in such an unfrequented place. The fact remains that Bernadette did find it and that this was no accident; she did so as a result of a direct command.[11]

On February 25, the crowd watched as Bernadette crawled on her hands and knees to the back of the grotto, where she dug in the ground and uncovered some muddy water. After several tries, she managed to drink some of it and smeared some on her face. When asked to explain her actions, she said that *aquero* had directed her to drink at the spring and to wash in it. Later that day, some people dug deeper at the spot where Bernadette had been digging, found a spring there, and **took bottles of the water back to Lourdes, suspecting it of possessing special powers.** By March 4, when Antoine Clarens, a cousin by marriage of Bernadette's father, wrote one of the first lengthy accounts of the events at the grotto, **cures were being attributed to water from this spring, and many people were carrying away samples of it.**[12]

---

11   Ibid., pp. 133,134.
12   *Encountering Mary*, p. 50.

Catholic doctrine and confidence in papal decrees have been strengthened by Lourdes and the healings that occurred there over the years.

Did *Jewish* Mary Turn into *a Mexican* in 1531 at Guadalupe?

Though the apparition at Guadalupe, Mexico might not be in the top three, it is still very significant, especially among Mexicans. According to the report, Mary appeared as a *young Mexican girl,* **who was dressed like an Aztec queen**, to the 57 year old Juan Diego:

> The sun wasn't above the horizon, yet Juan saw her as if against the sun because of the golden beams that rayed her person from head to feet. **She was a young Mexican girl about fourteen years old and wonderfully beautiful.**[13]

> The seer saw the Blessed Virgin **as a person of his own race,** and was firm in this conviction. Her physiognomy in the painting bears him out, as also do her garments. **Her star-studded outer mantle resembles that of an Aztec queen.**[14]

> Dear little son, I love you. I want you to know who I am. **I am the ever-virgin Mary, Mother of the true God who gives life and maintains it in existence.**[15]

> The Blessed Virgin said: "My little son. Do not be distressed and afraid. Am I not here who am **your Mother?** **Are you not under my shadow and protection?**...."[16]

---

13   *Woman*, p. 41.
14   Ibid., p. 59.
15   Ibid., p. 42.
16   Ibid., p. 49.

As with other Catholic sources, this apparition is declaring that Mary is a perpetual virgin, mother of God, mother of the Church and our *protection.* But this vision goes further with the *Mary of Catholicism* claiming to be the *giver of life* and maintaining its existence. Even if one might think it is somehow possible for the Jewish Mary to appear as a *Mexican girl,* anyone acquainted with the Bible will be greatly bothered by these others ideas.

Who is the real *giver of life*? Notice what the Bible says:

For the bread of God is **he** who comes down from heaven and **gives life to the world.** (John 6:33)

In the sight of **God, who gives life to everything**, and of Christ Jesus, who while testifying before Pontius Pilate made the good confession, I charge you (1 Tim 6:13)

Also, Heb. 1:3 tells us who is *sustaining all things*:

The Son is the radiance of God's glory and the exact representation of his being, **sustaining all things** by his powerful word. After he had provided purification for sins, he sat down at the right hand of the Majesty in heaven.

Especially disturbing to those who know the Bible's message is the thought that she is the one we are to rely upon for *protection.* God's word is crystal clear as it declares that **God is our *protection* and the like,** as already shown previously.

The Lady of the Miraculous Medal

At the age of 24, Catherine Laboure, who later became known as the "Saint of Ordinary People," had this apparition which resulted in a medal being made asking Mary to *pray for us:*

The first Marian apparition of the nineteenth century to receive widespread attention and to be formally recognized by Roman Catholic authorities was the apparition reported by **Catherine Laboure in the convent of the Sisters of Charity of St. Vincent de Paul on the Rue du Bac in Paris, in July and November of 1830.** The most important feature of this Rue du Bac apparition was the purported revelation of an image of the Virgin which Catherine said **she was instructed to have struck into a religious medal, over which was to be written the prayer, "O Mary, conceived without sin, pray for us who have recourse to thee." This medal began to be minted in 1832 and quickly became very popular.** While it is generally acknowledged that the great popularity of **this "Miraculous Medal" helped prepare the way for Pope Pius IX's proclamation of the dogma of the Immaculate Conception in 1854,** it would seem that it also contributed substantially to the Church's formal approval of the authenticity of Catherine's visions in 1836 and to **Catherine's beatification in 1933 and canonization in 1947.**[17]

Catherine saw a young boy with Mary, who she thought was her guardian angel and to whom she had *often prayed:*

> I believe that this child was my guardian angel, who showed himself that he might take me to see the Blessed Virgin, for **I had often prayed to him** to obtain this favor for me.[18]

The vision revealed the following to Catherine, which is also clear proof that Catholics do pray **to** angels as well as to Mary:

---

17   *Encountering Mary*, p. 26.
18   *Woman*, p. 71.

This made me realize how right it was to **pray to the Blessed Virgin** and how generous she was to those **who did pray to her**, what **graces she gave to those who asked for them**, what joy she had in giving them.[19]

This vision is saying that Mary is the *grace* dispenser. Furthermore, as with the Rosary and Brown Scapular, the *Miraculous medal* came about and/or became popular as a direct result from visions. The Miraculous medal is known as a *sacramental,* like the other two:

It is one of only three sacramentals in the history of the Church to be thus liturgically honored, sharing its distinction with **the Rosary and the Brown Scapular.**[20]

All visions are *questionable* and must be carefully examined with the Bible and flatly rejected, and even opposed, if they contain a contradictory message to Scripture, as this one does. This particular apparition paved the way for the *Immaculate Conception* papal decree which followed, which in turn has caused multitudes to trust in the *Mary of Catholicism.*

Fulfilled Prophecy

What about fulfilled prophecy? Doesn't this positively prove God would have to be behind these visions, as claimed by Catholic sources?

Our Lady does, however, **foretell the dire happenings to befall France and the world in 1870,** that year of turmoil and upheaval. There is some reason to believe that her predictions were not meant to apply only to the year 1870, for, during the revolution of 1830, which erupted just a

19   Ibid., p. 77.
20   Ibid., p. 84.

week after this apparition, and during the revolution of 1848, these predictions were fulfilled at least in part. It is an especially striking fact that, although Archbishop Darboy was murdered in 1870, as Our Lady had foretold, so too, Archbishop Affre was shot to death on the barricades in 1848, and Archbishop de Quelen had twice to flee for his life during the "Glorious Three Days" of the revolution of 1830. **The fulfillment of these terrible prophecies of the Mother of God may be considered in a practical way as grim proof of the authenticity of the visions.**[21]

Surprisingly fulfilled prophecy doesn't necessarily mean God is behind the vision! Please carefully note the following Scripture:

If a prophet, or one who **foretells** by dreams, appears among you and **announces to you a miraculous sign or wonder, and if the sign or wonder of which he has spoken takes place**, and he says, "Let us follow other gods" (gods you have not known) "and let us worship them," you must not listen to the words of that prophet or dreamer. **The LORD your God is testing you to find out whether you love him with all your heart and with all your soul. It is the LORD your God you must follow, and him you must revere. Keep his commands and obey him; serve him and hold fast to him.** (Deu 13:1-4)

Unless a person has read that passage, he would never think that the God of the Bible would allow **true prophecy** to be accompanied by a message including false worship or to follow a false god, as a *test* of our *love for* God, that is, **to see if we love God with all of our heart and soul or not, which would be shown by putting another before Him.**

---

21   Ibid., p. 74.

The Immaculate Conception of Mary

As with other Marian visions, the Lady of the Miraculous Medal also bolsters the support in an unscriptural belief—*the immaculate conception of Mary.*

"At this moment, I was so overjoyed that I no longer knew where I was. A frame, slightly oval in shape, formed round the Blessed Virgin. Within it was **written in letters of gold**:

"'**O Mary, conceived without sin**, pray for us who have recourse to thee.'

"The inscription, in a semi-circle, began at the height of the right hand, passed over the head, and finished at the height of the left hand.

"The golden ball disappeared in the brilliance of the sheaves of light bursting from all sides; the hands turned out and the arms were bent down under the weight of the treasures of grace obtained.

"Then the voice said:

"'Have a Medal struck after this model. **All who wear it will receive great graces**; they should **wear it around the neck. Graces will abound for those who wear it with confidence.'**

"At this instant the tableau seemed to me to turn, and I beheld the reverse of the Medal: a large M surmounted by a bar and a cross; beneath the M were the Hearts of Jesus and Mary, the one crowned with thorns, the other pierced with a sword."[22]

The spread of the Medal was so rapid and the flood of favors it let loose so startling, that the faithful gave it the name "Miraculous." The number of Medals minted

---

22   Ibid., p. 78.

since **1832**, when it was first struck, is beyond all counting. **It is easily in the hundreds of millions.** . . . Best of all, the Medal seems to have a special power for promoting and **deepening personal devotion to the Mother of God.**[23]

The message of this particular vision has *deepening personal devotion to the Mother of God* instead of pointing people to the Lord Jesus and glorifying him like the Holy Spirit does (John 16:13,14). But that is not all:

The prominent theological doctrine of the apparition is, of course, the Immaculate Conception. The proper name of the Medal is **the Medal of the Immaculate Conception,** and it was so called from the beginning until the people themselves, pleased with the wonders it worked, called it the Miraculous Medal. **The doctrine of the Immaculate Conception is symbolically portrayed in the representation of Mary crushing the head of the serpent, a reference to Genesis 3:15, "I will put enmities between thee and the woman, and thy seed and her seed; she shall crush thy head, and thou shalt lie in wait for her heel."** The doctrine is specifically mentioned in the golden letters which formed round the Virgin: "O Mary, conceived without sin . . ."[24]

This vision, among other things, is also a substantiation of the Catholic Bible's mistranslation of Genesis 3:15, which reads in part, *she shall crush thy head, and thou shalt lie in wait for her heel.* The Catholic Church cancels Jesus out of this verse of Scripture and replaces Him with Mary.

---

23   Ibid., pp. 84, 85.
24   Ibid., p. 82.

La Salette and Mary's Sabbath

On September 19, 1846 the apparition at La Salette was seen by two cattle herders, Melanie Mathieu, aged 14, and Maximin Giraud, aged 11:

> The apparition at La Salette, high in the French Alps near Grenoble, where in 1846 two shepherd children reported a single meeting with a figure assumed to be the Virgin Mary, was **the first Marian apparition of modern times outside of the cloistered religious environment to attract widespread attention and to be officially "recognized" by Roman Catholic authorities.**[25]

Once again, as found in other Catholic sources, this vision portrays **Mary as the one *protecting* us from angry Jesus.**

> **"If my people will not obey, I shall be compelled to loose my Son's arm. It is so heavy, so pressing that I can no longer restrain it.** How long I have suffered for you! If my Son is not to cast you off, I am obliged to entreat Him without ceasing. But you take no least notice of that. No matter how well you pray in future, no matter how well you act, you will never be able to make up to me what I have endured for your sake.
>
> **"I have appointed you six days for working. The seventh I have reserved for myself.** And no one will give it to me. This it is which causes the weight of my Son's arm to be so crushing. . . ."[26]

Shockingly, the personage in this vision claiming to be Mary spoke words similar to what God spoke in the following two verses:

---

25   *Encountering Mary*, p. 27.
26   *Woman*, p. 93.

Six days you shall labor and do all your work, but the seventh day **is a Sabbath to the LORD your God**. . . . (Ex 20:9,10)

The important difference between the Scriptures and the vision's message is the difference between truth and *idolatry.* Please know that **no Scripture states that the** *Mary of the Bible* **appointed six days for us to work, reserving the seventh for herself.** The truth is when God gave mankind Ex. 20:9,10, **Mary was not yet in existence. (The Catholic authorities seemingly had no problem endorsing this vision with this amazing falsehood regarding their Mary.)**

Furthermore, **the** *Mary of Catholicism* **is not holding back Jesus' arm (in judgment) nor is she capable of this, since she doesn't have the power to do so.** Again, Catholicism wrongly portrays their Mary as being more merciful than **Jesus** and **our protector**. We must remember, the Bible shows Jesus as being *merciful* to the poor, sick and the sinners **who came to him for mercy**, without any assistance from Mary at all. Also, the Jesus of the Bible is filled with *compassion* for those he encountered. See Mt. 9:36; 14:14; 15:32; 20:34; Mk. 1:41; 6:34; 8:2; etc. The Bible's message is vastly different than the picture we get from these Marian visions, as well as from other Catholic sources.

Mary's Prophecy at La Salette

This is what the *Mary of Catholicism* said:

If the harvest is spoiled, it is your fault. I warned you last year about the potatoes, but you have not heeded it. On the contrary, when you found the potatoes had spoiled you swore and you introduced the name of my son. **They will**

continue this year so that by Christmas there will be none left.[27]

Please see the aforementioned explanation under *The Lady of the Miraculous medal* for an answer to fulfilled prophecy like this.

La Salette's Healing Water

One of the best known reported healings that occurred as a result of this apparition, was the following one:

A particular well known **healing attributed to La Salette's water** was that of Marie Laurent, of Corps. She had been disabled for some twenty-three years, suffering first from rheumatic pains and then from injuries incurred by falls, and for about sixteen years she had been unable to move without crutches. She reportedly made some soup from water drawn from the spring and drank this each day during a novena which began on November 17. By November 24, she felt well enough, it was said, to go to confession without her crutches, and the next day, to Communion. Melin, in reporting this cure to the bishop on December 2, said that at that time the woman was still weak but that she was so pleased with her recovery that she was forgetting to eat.[28]

Moreover, **in the Scriptures, people who sought *mercy* and went directly to Jesus or to God, received *mercy*,** unlike the impression one would get from the *Mary of La Salette*. Jesus never sent any person away to go to Mary first, to then have her bring that person back to him. Please notice that Jesus or the Heavenly Father showed *mercy* to all of the following people

---

27   *Encountering Mary*, p. 30.
28   Ibid., p. 37.

who were in need of healing, salvation, etc. This was done without Mary *interceding* for the ones in need:

> As Jesus went on from there, two blind men followed him, calling out, **"Have mercy on us, Son of David!"** (Mat 9:27)

> A Canaanite woman from that vicinity came to him, crying out, **"Lord, Son of David, have mercy on me!** My daughter is suffering terribly from demon-possession." (Mat 15:22)

> **"Lord, have mercy on my son,"** he said. "He has seizures and is suffering greatly. He often falls into the fire or into the water. . . ." (Mat 17:15)

> Two blind men were sitting by the roadside, and when they heard that Jesus was going by, they shouted, **"Lord, Son of David, have mercy on us!"** (Mat 20:30)

> The crowd rebuked them and told them to be quiet, but they shouted all the louder, **"Lord, Son of David, have mercy on us!"** (Mat 20:31)

> Jesus did not let him, but said, "Go home to your family and tell them how much **the Lord** has done for you, and how **he has had mercy on you.**" (Mark 5:19)

> When he heard that it was Jesus of Nazareth, he began to shout, **"Jesus, Son of David, have mercy on me!"** (Mark 10:47)

> Many rebuked him and told him to be quiet, but he shouted all the more, **"Son of David, have mercy on me!"** (Mark 10:48)

But the tax collector stood at a distance. He would not even look up to heaven, but beat his breast and said, "**God, have mercy on me, a sinner.**" (Luke 18:13)

He called out, "**Jesus, Son of David, have mercy on me!**" (Luke 18:38)

Those who led the way rebuked him and told him to be quiet, but he shouted all the more, "**Son of David, have mercy on me!**" (Luke 18:39)

For God has bound all men over to disobedience **so that he may have mercy on them all.** (Rom 11:32)

Therefore, I urge you, brothers, **in view of God's mercy,** to offer your bodies as living sacrifices, holy and pleasing to God—this is your spiritual act of worship. (Rom 12:1)

Indeed he was ill, and almost died. But **God had mercy on him**, and not on him only but also on me, to spare me sorrow upon sorrow. (Phil 2:27)

To Timothy my true son in the faith: **Grace, mercy and peace from God the Father and Christ Jesus our Lord.** (1 Tim 1:2)

To Timothy, my dear son: **Grace, mercy and peace from God the Father and Christ Jesus our Lord.** (2 Tim 1:2)

he saved us, not because of righteous things we had done, but **because of his mercy**. He saved us through the washing of rebirth and renewal by the Holy Spirit, (Titus 3:5)

Let us then approach the throne of grace with confidence, so **that we may receive mercy and find grace to help us in our time of need.** (Heb 4:16)

As you know, we consider blessed those who have persevered. You have heard of Job's perseverance and have seen what the Lord finally brought about. **The Lord is full of compassion and mercy**. (James 5:11)

Praise be to the God and **Father** of our Lord Jesus Christ! **In his great mercy** he has given us new birth into a living hope through the resurrection of Jesus Christ from the dead, (1 Pet 1:3)

Grace, mercy and peace from God the Father and from Jesus Christ, the Father's Son, will be with us in truth and love. (2 John 1:3)

In Bible days, people in distress called out to the Heavenly Father or the Lord Jesus and found the *mercy* they were looking for. If it worked for them, why should we think such won't work for us today? Many other Scriptures could also be cited.

It has been asked *what are these messages*, in reference to the Marian visions. After all of the aforementioned, the answer is apparent: **All of the Marian apparitions magnify Catholic doctrine and especially *the Mary of Catholicism*—pointing people to *trust her* for help, protection, healing, salvation, etc.** By doing so, many sincere-but-Scripturally-misled people are pointed away from the Lord, the true and only source of help and salvation. Hence, sincere people are not finding the mercy, protection or salvation they long for. This is the consequence of being deceived in this manner. Multitudes of precious souls hang in the balance and are in the greatest spiritual danger—that of being lost, unless they learn the truth before it is too late.♥

14

Miracles—Two Sources

When one reads through the book of Revelation, he can easily see that the terminal generation of this age will see and/or personally experience the effects of war, famine, martyrdom, gross sin and deceit through *Satanic miracles*! Unfortunately, many people in our day don't recognize that **miracles do come through two sources—God and the devil! Hence, they are open for demonic deception.**

In the book of Exodus, we learn that **some of God's miracles were duplicated by Satan's power channeled through the Egyptian magicians: a wooden staff became a snake (7:10,11); water was changed into blood (7:20-22) and frogs came out of the water and covered the land (8:6,7)!**

Demons can and do perform *miraculous signs*:

> They are **spirits of demons performing miraculous signs**, and they go out to the kings of the whole world, to gather them for the battle on the great day of God Almighty. (Rev 16:14)

To be specific, we can be sure that our generation, if it is the last generation, will hear of or see in the future **fire coming down from Heaven to earth and an image of the Antichrist speaking because of Satanic power:**

163

And he performed **great and miraculous signs**, even caus-
ing **fire to come down from heaven to earth in full view
of men**. (Rev 13:13)

**He was given power to give breath to the image of the
first beast, so that it could speak** and cause all who refused to worship the image to be killed. (Rev 13:15)

In fact, it will be because of such *miracles* **that the ones
who receive the mark of the beast and worship his image will
be deceived:**

But the beast was captured, and with him **the false prophet who had performed the miraculous signs on his
behalf. With these signs he had deluded those who had
received the mark of the beast and worshiped his
image**. The two of them were thrown alive into the fiery
lake of burning sulfur. (Rev 19:20)

Please read and circle that verse in your own Bible for
yourself. The people who receive the mark of the beast will be
deceived by astounding and awe-inspiring *miracles* produced by
Satanic power!
Also ponder 2 Thess. 2:9,10:

The coming of the lawless one will be in accordance with
**the work of Satan displayed in all kinds of counterfeit
miracles, signs and wonders**, and in every sort of evil that
deceives those who are perishing. They perish because they
refused to love the truth and so be saved.

Some people wrongly think the devil is in Hell now. Instead, the Bible shows he travels around the earth looking for
someone to *devour*:

Be self-controlled and alert. **Your enemy the devil prowls around like a roaring lion looking for someone to devour.** (1 Pet 5:8)

The devil is such a good deceiver that we need the full armor of God to stand against his *schemes*:

Put on the full armor of God so that you can take your stand against **the devil's schemes.** (Eph 6:11)

Satan has in the past, is now and will continue in the future to use *miracles* to deceive. This truth is the answer to the mystic questions regarding Edgar Cayce, Padre Pio, etc. who carried conflicting messages about God and the afterlife along with their signs and miracles.

Similar conflicting messages surrounding miracles and visions are found in a comparison of Mormonism and Catholicism. For example, after prayer, the Mormons were saved by sea gulls which ate the crickets that were eating their grain in Brigham Young's day.

In contrast, the Catholic church endorsed with the highest honors the 1917 Fatima visions of a personage claiming to be the Virgin Mary, which declared herself as our *refuge* and *the way that will lead you to God.* Such is in direct conflict with Jn. 14:6 and other Scriptures, which declare Jesus as the only *way* to God!

Since Mormonism and Catholicism both have miracles and visions and their messages about salvation are in conflict with each other, we logically know that God can't be the only power source for these miracles and visions. We can be dogmatic, since God is not a God of confusion. [God's power was not active in either of these cases!]

What then must we gauge all messages and teachings by, since miracles, visions, signs, etc. can be produced by the devil and therefore be deceptive? The criterion is God's un-

changing written word (2 Tim.3:16,17). If God's word isn't considered as final authority when *testing* a miracle, vision, dream, prophecy, teaching, etc., one will probably be deceived and could possibly lose his soul! Did you know that if you are deceived by a miracle into receiving the mark of the beast, you will end up in Hell, even if you were once saved?

> A third angel followed them and said in a loud voice: "If **anyone** worships the beast and his image and receives his mark on the forehead or on the hand, he, too, will drink of the wine of God's fury, which has been poured full strength into the cup of his wrath. **He will be tormented with burning sulfur in the presence of the holy angels and of the Lamb. And the smoke of their torment rises for ever and ever. There is no rest day or night for those who worship the beast and his image, or for anyone who receives the mark of his name." This calls for patient endurance on the part of the saints who obey God's commandments and remain faithful to Jesus.** (Rev 14:9–12)

We must be both *self-controlled* and *alert* to stand against the devil and his wiles (1 Pet 5:8; Eph. 6:10,11). To reflect upon the contents of this message until an indelible impression is made upon your mind might make a difference in your eternity beyond the grave! Remember, these are perilous days that call for discernment.

In conclusion, God still performs miracles in our day (Jn.14:12; Acts 4:30; etc.), but so does the devil (2 Cor. 11:14; Rev. 16:14; 2 Thess. 2:9,10; etc.)! When God's power is behind a miracle, it will point people to the message of the Bible where Jesus is exalted as the only *mediator* and the only *way* to the Father.♥

15

The Real Mary Of The Bible

The Bible has many praiseworthy things to report about the real Mary, the mother of the Lord Jesus. Because of the many distortions and misrepresentations she has been labeled with, many non-Catholics have never really studied her with admiration. Let's now take a close-up look at the real Mary, the *mother of Jesus* (Acts 1:14):

The Facts

1. **She was a very godly woman, who was *blessed among women* (Lk. 1:42) to be uniquely privileged to bear the Savior of the world.** She was chosen by God to bear the Redeemer. She humbly described herself as God's *handmaiden* (Lk. 1:48, KJV), which is another way of saying she was a *servant* or *slave* for the LORD.

2. **She was willing to risk her own life to obey God** and become impregnated with Jesus, for in those days *adultery* would be punished by stoning to death (Lev. 20:10), which is what it would appear she was guilty of, though she was innocent. **Hence, she was going to serve God to the point of death, regardless the cost.**

3.   **She was willing to imperil her marriage with Joseph, by her obedience to God,** as it certainly did until Joseph had a dream from God regarding this situation (Mt. 1:18-20). That saved their marriage!

4.   **She was also ready to be the topic of slanderous, untrue gossip and evil suspicion by those who would see her pregnant.** Such untrue words can be crushing to the innocent and conscientious (Job 19:2), such as Mary.

5.   **She was also a person of great faith.** Mary was still a *virgin* at that point, since she and Joseph never had sexual contact until after Jesus was born (Mt. 1:25), yet **Mary had faith to believe for the impossible.**

6.   Without a doubt, after Jesus and Mary's other children were born, (Joseph and) Mary raised them, in the ways of God, since they were both godly themselves. **With Joseph being the head of the household, Mary certainly followed his godly leadership, which benefitted their entire family (and marriage).**

7.   After Jesus started his earthly ministry at the age of 30, Mary is to be commended again as she told the people at the wedding at Cana:

"Do whatever he tells you." (John 2:5)

     In other words, she knew that Jesus had the answers for life's problems. Simple obedience to God's word is exalted here, even if it doesn't always make sense in the natural. **The Mary of the Bible pointed people *away from herself to the teachings and directives of Jesus. She also encouraged us to have faith in Jesus and not in herself.***

8. **Mary was at the foot of the cross mourning and sympathizing with the other disciples over the harsh and unfair treatment given to her *firstborn* (Lk. 2:7), as he alone paid the price for our redemption.** This was a dangerous time to be associated with Jesus, yet she (and other disciples) were there at the cross grieving over what wicked and ignorant people did to him.

9. **After the ascension of the Lord Jesus into Heaven, she was in the upper room patiently awaiting to be filled and empowered with the Holy Spirit along with the other 120 disciples.** We, however, never see her afterwards doing any exploits or miracles in the name of the Lord, as the other disciples did in the book of Acts, who were also filled with the Holy Spirit at the same time she was.

Additional Truths Related to Mary

A. While Mary was blessed *among* women, as already stated, **Scripture does not say she was blessed *above* women.** Furthermore, she being *blessed* in this manner is not unique to her alone. Jael is described in a similar fashion. Notice the following:

> Blessed above women shall Jael the wife of Heber the Kenite be, **blessed shall she be above women** in the tent. (Judg 5:24, KJV)

There are also many others who are described as *blessed.* Just one such example is shown in James:

> **Blessed** is the man who perseveres under trial, because when he has stood the test, he will receive the crown of life that God has promised to those who love him. (James 1:12)

Furthermore, according to Jesus himself **John the Baptist was *greater* than Mary:**

> I tell you the truth: Among those born of women **there has not risen anyone greater than John the Baptist** .... (Mat 11:11)

Moreover, **Jesus told us who is *the greatest in the kingdom of heaven,* but did not say it was Mary:**

> Therefore, whoever humbles himself like this child is the **greatest** in the kingdom of heaven. (Mat 18:4)

B. While it is certainly true that Jesus did what his mother requested at Cana, it is also true that **the Lord equally responded to the wishes of others at times,** which also resulted in the **miraculous:**

> While he was saying this, a ruler came and knelt before him and said, "My daughter has just died. **But come** and put your hand on her, and she will live." **Jesus got up and went with him,** and so did his disciples ... After the crowd had been put outside, he went in and **took the girl by the hand, and she got up.** (Mat 9:18,19, 25)

Hence, in light of this passage, the miracle at Cana has been misused and distorted to teach we can go to Mary to get her to uniquely move the hand of the Lord in our behalf—meaning that she has a special ability and closeness to the Lord to do this. **The truth is: The real *Mary of the Bible* doesn't have a unique influence on the Lord Jesus to affect his actions.**

The Lord Refused Mary

Also remember that at least one time, **the Lord** *denied* **Mary's request to talk to him:**

> While Jesus was still talking to the crowd, **his mother** and brothers stood outside, **wanting to speak to him.** Someone told him, "Your mother and brothers are standing outside, wanting to speak to you." He replied to him, **"Who is my mother, and who are my brothers?"** Pointing to his disciples, he said, **"Here are my mother and my brothers. For whoever does the will of my Father in heaven is my brother and sister and mother."** (Mat 12:46-50)

C.   **While Mary was certainly a godly mother and wife, this doesn't mean she was the perfect mother.** Evidence for this appears as she neglected to care for Jesus when she and Joseph returned from the Passover in Jerusalem. She didn't know the boy Jesus (only 12 years of age) was not in their company until a full day went by:

> Thinking he was in their company, **they traveled on for a day.** Then they began looking for him among their relatives and friends. (Luke 2:44)

Since Joseph and Mary traveled for a full day before discovering Jesus wasn't with them, it took another day for them to return to Jerusalem, which means Jesus was left alone with no apparent place to sleep or food to eat during those two days. Then it took another three days to find him (Lk. 2:46).

How could Mary (and Joseph) forget about Jesus as they returned home from a distant place, especially if he was their only child? Is such possible for a couple with only one child? On the other hand, Scripture shows Jesus had multiple brothers and sisters in his natural family, while he was still the *firstborn* (or oldest). (See our chapter entitled, *Mary's Virginity*.) A possible reason for this negligence is that Joseph and Mary were busy tending to the many needs of their other children, who were all younger and much more dependent than he was. Whatever the reason, **they were so preoccupied that they neglected to check the health and well-being of the boy Jesus.**

The Catholic Dilemma

D. **For a Christian to reject the perpetual virginity of Mary, as taught by Catholicism, is no real insult to her.** In fact, for a married woman (including Mary) to remain a virgin after being married, is unscriptural:

> But since there is so much immorality, each man should have his own wife, and each woman her own husband. The husband should fulfill his marital duty to his wife, and likewise **the wife to her husband. The wife's body does not belong to her alone but also to her husband.** In the same way, the husband's body does not belong to him alone but also to his wife. (1 Cor 7:2-4)

So now will the devout Catholic *deny Mary's sinlessness,* because she violated this command to sexually unite with Joseph or *repudiate her perpetual virginity,* as declared by Catholicism? This is a small part of the problem that Catholicism has created for itself by going beyond Scripture to create a Mary that doesn't exist and is trusted in for deliverance and salvation. **Again, the evidence shows that the *Mary of Catholicism* is not the *Mary of the Bible*, but a dangerous distortion that has led multitudes into *idolatry* and *a false salvation hope.***

E. Though Mary had great faith to believe she could get pregnant while still a virgin, this doesn't mean others didn't have greater faith than she did. **In fact, many are men-**

tioned in the faith chapter (Hebrews 11) as the examples of faith, yet Mary is excluded from the list.

F. While Mary had godly wisdom this doesn't mean that she
was beyond being deceived herself. This is apparent since
**she actually thought Jesus was *out of his mind* at a point
in time during his ministry:**

When his **family** heard about this, they went to take charge
of him, **for they said, "He is out of his mind."** ...**Then
Jesus' mother and brothers arrived.** Standing outside,
they sent someone in to call him. A crowd was sitting
around him, and they told him, **"Your mother and brothers are outside looking for you."** "Who are my mother
and my brothers?" he asked. Then he looked at those
seated in a circle around him and said, **"Here are my
mother and my brothers! Whoever does God's will is
my brother and sister and mother."** Again Jesus began
to teach by the lake. The crowd that gathered around him
was so large that he got into a boat and sat in it out on the
lake, while all the people were along the shore at the
water's edge. (Mark 3:21-4:1)

This is another passage which shows that the Lord denied
Mary's request! Furthermore, **Jesus placed any person who
does the will of God on a par with the real Mary, as is apparent in that passage. The *Mary of the Bible* is not superior to
any such person, according to Jesus himself.** In fact, the Lord
would have us all know that Mary does not have a special role
or blessing upon her because she gave birth to Jesus:

As Jesus was saying these things, a woman in the crowd
called out, "Blessed is the mother who gave you birth and
nursed you." He replied, "Blessed rather are **those who
hear the word of God and obey it**." (Luke 11:27,28)

Notice: Jesus publicly rebuked the woman praising Mary because she gave birth to Jesus and went on to state who the real *blessed* people are—*those who hear the word of God and obey it.*

Another Glimpse at the *Mary of the Bible*

Jesus called Mary *woman* (John 2:4; 19:26) the same Greek word he used at other times for other females with no special attachment to him:

> When Jesus saw her, he called her forward and said to her, "**Woman**, you are set free from your infirmity." (Lk 13:12)

> Then Jesus answered, "**Woman**, you have great faith! Your request is granted." And her daughter was healed from that very hour. (Matt 15:28)

By calling Mary by the *same* term that others were also called, the Lord showed he was not favorably disposed towards his mother the way Catholicism states him to be. Jesus *honored* his mother, but not as Catholicism presents it and all disciples of the Lord are on a par with her, according to Jesus himself (Mt. 12:49,50; Lk. 11:27,28).

Finally, please remember the post-ascended Jesus in Rev. 1 was not a baby or child and Mary wasn't with him. It is not a Son/mother team. Never is Mary shown to be a *Queen* in the book of Revelation, nor is she even mentioned one time. **These truths are not an attack on the *Mary of the Bible*, but instead, an exposé and refutation of the counterfeit *Mary of Catholicism* that has led people away from trusting Jesus alone for salvation.**

Conclusion

We know the *Mary of the Bible* was very godly, willing to risk her life as well as her future marriage and be the topic of slanderous gossip to obey God. She also had faith to believe for the impossible, submitted to her husband in the Lord, raised her children in the truth of God, **pointed people away from herself to the teachings and directives of Jesus,** mourned at the foot of the cross for the way Jesus was treated as he was dying, and waited patiently in the upper room for the Holy Spirit with the other 120. **Yet all of this is only a small part of the whole picture we have about her. To only magnify the former truths, to the exclusion of the others, will mislead precious souls into idolatry and a false plan of salvation.** This is what Catholicism has done in their excesses about Mary.

These additional Scriptures about Mary have been suppressed and ignored by many who have exalted her to the reigning Queen of the Universe. Just because Mary was chosen over all other women to bear Jesus doesn't justify elevating her to the place where she has a role in one's salvation or even thinking she is specially *blessed* (Lk. 11:27,28). **In fact, to place any trust in Mary for your salvation is to disobey the many commands in Scripture to trust in Jesus alone. Hence, if one is not placing his submissive faith in Jesus, he is *without salvation* and in *disobedience to God.* This is why this information is so important. The evidence is overwhelmingly clear that multitudes of sincere Catholics have been misled by their own spiritual leaders, past and present, regarding *salvation* itself.**

Though Mary is a primary figure in Catholicism, there is much more information in God's word about other servants of God, such as Moses, Abraham, the apostle Paul, etc. Unlike others, she never wrote part of the Bible or died a martyr of the faith. Furthermore, absolutely no scripture states: That we are to go to Mary to get to Jesus, that she is a co-redeemer, or that she is to be prayed to, trusted in or venerated. **The real Mary of the Bible is the Christian's sister, not his mother.** (See our chapter entitled, *Is Mary The Mother of the Church?*)♥

16 ━━━━━━━━━━━━━━━━━━━━━━━━━━━

Titles And Names Of Jesus

The whole Bible is filled with references to Jesus in one way or another. Beyond that, the primary message spread by the Lord Himself and his followers was *to go directly to Jesus Himself, place a submissive-obedient faith/trust in him, deny yourself and faithfully continue [endure] to the end for salvation.* It is very easy to see why we are directed by God to do this after noting the various ways the Lord Jesus is described by his many names and titles. Each refers to yet another important place or position that Jesus holds in God's plan for man's salvation. Please ponder how precious and preeminently important Jesus is for man's salvation. **The truth is: Jesus is the all-sufficient Savior. No other** *savior* **is needed besides Him or with Him.** (Please know that the following is just **a partial listing** of the many Scriptural names and titles of the Lord, each reflecting a special role or function Jesus has in the plan of salvation, creation, etc.)

Advocate (1 John 2:1)
Almighty (Rev. 1:8; Mt. 28:18)
Alpha and Omega (Rev. 1:8; 22:13)
Amen (Rev. 3:14)
Apostle of our Profession (Heb. 3:1)
Atoning Sacrifice for our Sins (1 John 2:2)

Author of Life (Acts 3:15)
Author and Perfecter of our Faith (Heb. 12:2)
Author of Salvation (Heb. 2:10)
Beginning and End (Rev. 22:13)
Blessed and only Ruler (1 Tim. 6:15)
Bread of God (John 6:33)
Bread of Life (John 6:35; 6:48)
Capstone (Acts 4:11; 1 Pet. 2:7)
Chief Cornerstone (Eph. 2:20)
Chief Shepherd (1 Pet. 5:4)
Christ (1 John 2:22)
Creator (John 1:3)
Deliverer (Rom. 11:26)
Eternal Life (1 John 1:2; 5:20)
Everlasting Father (Isa. 9:6)
Gate (John 10:9)
Faithful and True (Rev. 19:11)
Faithful Witness (Rev. 1:5)
Faithful and True Witness (Rev. 3:14)
First and Last (Rev. 1:17; 2:8; 22:13)
Firstborn From the Dead (Rev. 1:5)
God (John 1:1; 20:28; Heb. 1:8; Rom. 9:5; 2 Pet. 1:1;1 John
    5:20; etc.)
Good Shepherd (John 10:11,14)
Great Shepherd (Heb. 13:20)
Great High Priest (Heb. 4:14)
Head of the Church (Eph. 1:22; 4:15; 5:23)
Heir of all things (Heb. 1:2)
High Priest (Heb. 2:17)
Holy and True (Rev. 3:7)
Holy One (Acts 3:14)
Hope (1 Tim. 1:1)
Hope of Glory (Col. 1:27)
Horn of Salvation (Luke 1:69)
I Am (John 8:58)

Image of God (2 Cor. 4:4)
King Eternal (1 Tim. 1:17)
King of Israel (John 1:49)
King of the Jews (Mt. 27:11)
King of kings (1 Tim 6:15; Rev. 19:16)
King of the Ages (Rev. 15:3)
Lamb (Rev. 13:8)
Lamb of God (John 1:29)
Lamb Without Blemish (1 Pet. 1:19)
Last Adam (1 Cor. 15:45)
Life (John 14:6; Col. 3:4)
Light of the World (John 8:12)
Lion of the Tribe of Judah (Rev. 5:5)
Living One (Rev. 1:18)
Living Stone (1 Pet. 2:4)
Lord (2 Pet. 2:20)
Lord of All (Acts 10:36)
Lord of Glory (1 Cor. 2:8)
Lord of lords (Rev. 19:16)
LORD [YHWH] our Righteousness (Jer. 23:6)
Man from Heaven (1 Cor. 15:48)
Mediator of the New Covenant (Heb. 9:15)
Mighty God (Isa. 9:6)
Morning Star (Rev. 22:16)
Offspring of David (Rev. 22:16)
Only Begotten Son of God (John 1:18; 1 John 4:9)
Our Great God and Savior (Titus 2:13)
Our Holiness (1 Cor. 1:30)
Our Husband (2 Cor. 11:2)
Our Protection (2 Thess. 3:3)
Our Redemption (1 Cor. 1:30)
Our Righteousness (1 Cor. 1:30)
Our Sacrificed Passover Lamb (1 Cor. 5:7)
Power of God (1 Cor. 1:24)
Precious Cornerstone (1 Pet. 2:6)

Prince of Peace (Isa. 9:6)
Prophet (Acts 3:22)
Resurrection and Life (John 11:25)
Righteous Branch (Jer. 23:5)
Righteous One (Acts 7:52; 1 John 2:1)
Rock (1 Cor. 10:4)
Root of David (Rev. 5:5; 22:16)
Ruler of God's Creation (Rev. 3:14)
Ruler of the Kings of the Earth (Rev. 1:5)
Savior (Eph. 5:23; Titus 1:4; 3:6; 2 Pet. 2:20)
Son of David (Lk. 18:39)
Son of God (John 1:49; Heb. 4:14)
Son of Man (Mt. 8:20)
Son of the Most High God (Lk. 1:32)
Source of eternal salvation for all who obey him (Heb. 5:9)
The One Mediator (1 Tim. 2:5)
The Stone the builders rejected (Acts 4:11)
True Bread (John 6:32)
True Light (John 1:9)
True Vine (John 15:1)
Truth (John 1:14; 14:6)
Way (John 14:6)
Wisdom of God (1 Cor. 1:24)
Wonderful Counselor (Isa. 9:6)
Word (John 1:1)
Word of God (Rev. 19:13)

JESUS can be fully trusted and relied upon 100% for our personal salvation and much more. There is no surer source of truth, for he himself is the *truth* and only way to God (John 14:6). **Yet, as the Bible exalts Jesus from cover to cover, Catholicism indirectly downplays him by their unscriptural exaltations of the Mary they have fabricated.** This is especially portrayed in Marian apparitions, pictures and/or statues where she is holding the baby Jesus in her arms as both wear a golden crown. The *Mary of Catholicism* is the mature adult and Jesus is just the infant held and dependent on his mother's help and strength.

Furthermore, without Scriptural backing, Catholicism also sometimes gives Mary **the same exact titles** which belong to Jesus alone—*Life, Hope, the Way, Advocate,* etc. **In fact, Catholicism has given their Mary more titles than the Bible has for the Lord Jesus, thus reflecting her importance to them in comparison to Jesus.** See Appendix B. Please remember: **the** *Mary of Catholicism* **isn't the** *Mary of the Bible*, but instead a sinless, queen of heaven, who has been bodily assumed there and supposedly is the life, hope, way to God, refuge and protection for multitudes. Many Catholics have even *consecrated* themselves to that Mary. **Hence, there are multitudes of sincere Catholics who have been innocently misled by their own teachers and leaders about Christianity and** *salvation*. **They are trusting in: (1) Mary or (2) Jesus and Mary (sacraments, church membership) for salvation, as they have been directed, instead of Jesus alone, as their own Bibles declare. Remember this: the Scriptures have been given to make us wise unto** *salvation* **through faith in Christ Jesus (2 Tim. 3:15-17). Therefore, even though many Catholics are sincere and devout, they are also in** *disobedience* **to Jesus' commands and the Apostles' directives regarding salvation.**

The Real Christian

Jesus wants all to know who his real spiritual family is. He said of them that they put God's word into *practice*, **which includes both obedience and having** *Jesus as the object of their faith for salvation*. **This is the foundational difference between a Catholic (as well as all other religious but unsaved people) and a Bible-defined Christian:**

He replied, "**My mother and brothers are those who hear God's word and put it into practice.**" (Luke 8:21)

For all Catholics who wisely decide to reject what they have been taught by the priests, nuns, bishops, popes, etc. and go by the eternal word of God instead, remember the following: You need to leave the Catholic church just as a Mormon needs to leave Mormonism after getting saved and a Muslim needs to leave Islam after becoming a child of God. *Catholicism is not the same as Biblical Christianity.* You need to gather with other true Christians, be spiritually fed and worship God in spirit and in truth. Be sure to read our important article entitled, *Vital Truths for New Converts* at www.evangelicaloutreach.ort/newconverts.htm

May God be pleased to use this chapter to open up the spiritual eyes of many Catholics to this dangerous, deadly *salvation* deception before it is too late. (Please pass these important truths on to your Catholic friends and relatives. Precious souls hang in the balance.) God bless you. (Be assured this chapter, as well as this entire book, was written out of Christian love for all who want to know about Biblical salvation.)♥

17

God's True Plan Of Salvation

The true plan of salvation is concisely stated in the Bible as repentance towards God and faith in Christ Jesus:

I have declared to both Jews and Greeks that **they must turn to God in repentance and have faith in our Lord Jesus**. (Acts 20:21)

To *repent* means **to turn from your evil ways** (Mat. 12:41 cf. Jonah 3:10). We are to produce fruit in keeping with repentance (Mat. 3:8) and prove our repentance by our deeds:

First to those in Damascus, then to those in Jerusalem and in all Judea, and to the Gentiles also, I preached that they should repent and turn to God and **prove their repentance by their deeds**. (Acts 26:20)

Every tree that does not bring forth good fruit will be cut down and thrown into the fire (Mat. 3:10; 7:19). The Lord Jesus also taught the road to life is *hard* and only a *few* will find it:

Enter by the narrow gate; for wide *is* the gate and broad *is* the way that leads to destruction, and there are many who go in by it. Because narrow *is* the gate and **difficult *is* the**

way which leads to life, and there are few who find it. (Mat 7:13,14, NKJV)

The Lord declared that there are only 2 gates, 2 roads, 2 groups of people and 2 eternal destinies. So don't follow the crowd, since they are on their way to eternal fire, even though they might not know it. Moreover, many get saved, but afterwards *fall away* (Lk. 8:13; Jn. 6:66; 1 Tim. 1:19; etc.). In other words, after initial salvation we must faithfully endure to the *end* to enter the Kingdom of God and escape the lake of fire (Mat. 10:22; Heb. 3:14; Rev. 2:10,11). Eternal life comes to the repentant the moment such believe on Jesus for salvation (Jn. 3:16; 6:47; 1 Jn. 5:12,13), but there is another important aspect of eternal life that many are totally unaware of in our day. According to true, Biblical, grace teaching, eternal life is also a hope (Titus 3:7), yet to be reaped (Gal. 6:8,9) in the age to come (Mk. 10:30) for only the ones who persist in doing good (Rom. 2:7) and do not grow weary and give up (Gal. 6:9).

Eternal life is more important than money, a love relationship, friends, fame, popularity, power or gaining the whole world. Do not forfeit your soul for these things:

What good is it for a man to gain the whole world, yet forfeit his soul? (Mk 8:36)

Your salvation is as important as eternity is long! Your faithfulness to Christ now (or lack of it) will affect you one hundred years from now and throughout the rest of eternity. People have spent time in prison, lost their jobs, spouses, friends, family, material possessions, lives, etc. to get salvation or retain their salvation. **You might have to pay the same price before your life, which is a "test," is over (Rev. 2:10,11)! You are battling for eternity—for your eternal soul and the souls of others!** Come to God on His terms and remain faithful to Him. This is the most important thing you will ever do in this life. Jesus said:

> **Make every effort to enter through the narrow door**, because many, I tell you, will try to enter and will **not** be able to. (Lk 13:24)

Keep yourself pure (1 Tim. 5:22), from idols (1 Jn. 5:21), from being polluted by the world (Jam. 1:27), and avoid every kind of evil (1 Thess. 5:22). Hold loosely to the things of this life, for they are all temporary. **Resist sinful temptations. Be on your guard against false teachers** (Jehovah's Witnesses, Mormons, eternal security teachers, ecumenical leaders, etc.). **Also, do not just accept what you hear from so-called Christian TV, radio, pulpits or Christian books! Much of what is taught through these channels is partly true and partly false. Some of it is pure poison for your soul. Verify everything you hear or read with Scripture taken in context. If it isn't found in the Bible, reject it! Compare Scripture with Scripture and consider everything in the Bible on the subject. Get a good, reliable and easy-to-read Bible translation. Study it for yourself. Don't just trust another's interpretation.**

Also, remember this: If a saved person sows to please his sinful nature he'll die spiritually (Rom. 8:13; Gal. 6:8,9; James 1:14-16). The prodigal is a clear example of this (Lk. 15:24,32). The end result of sin is spiritual death. Do not be deceived by the eternal security teachers who teach otherwise. **We must continue to unashamedly and faithfully follow Jesus to the end of our lives to enter the Kingdom of God:**

> All men will hate you because of me, but **he who stands firm to the end will be saved**. (Mat 10:22)

> If anyone is ashamed of me and my words, **the Son of Man will be ashamed of him** when he comes in his glory and in the glory of the Father and of the holy angels. (Lk 9:26)

Do not be afraid of what you are about to suffer. I tell you, the devil will put some of you in prison to test you, and you will suffer persecution for ten days. **Be faithful, even to the point of death**, and I will give you the crown of life. He who has an ear, let him hear what the Spirit says to the churches. **He who overcomes will not be hurt at all by the second death**. (Rev 2:10,11)

Jesus described his *sheep* as his *followers* (John 10:27). James stated that faith without [good] works is *dead* (James 2:17).

In conclusion, the Jesus of our present hour is not a baby that is laying in a manger or an infant that needs to be held in his mother's arms. He is an adult who successfully destroyed the devil's work (1 John 3:8). He is the resurrected *Lord of glory* (1 Cor. 2:8), before whom every knee will bow and every tongue confess that he is Lord (Phil. 2:9-11). Jesus has the only name in which salvation is found (Acts 4:12), is the only mediator between God and man (1 Tim. 2:5) and is the judge of the living and the dead (Acts 10:42; 2 Tim. 4:1; 1 Pet. 4:5). **We are advised in Scripture to go directly to Him for forgiveness by turning from sins, trusting in Him alone for our soul's salvation and remaining faithful to the very end.♥**

1

2

3

4

5

6

7

8

9

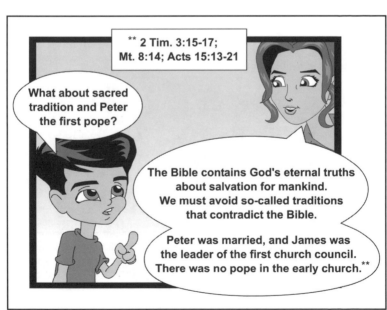

10

11

12

13

14

15

16

17

18

More Related Information

Many Catholics needlessly continue in unscriptural ways (praying to Mary, believing in Purgatory, attending mass, bowing before images, wearing the brown scapular, etc.) because they have never taken the time to sincerely seek out the truth, as declared in the Bible. However, for the ones that have and acted upon the word of God, there is salvation and forgiveness of sins. Dear reader, if you are a Catholic, what could be wrong with going directly to the actual teachings of the Lord Jesus and his apostles, as found in the Bible, and acting on them above all others?

Sincerity alone will not bring about salvation. There are many sincere but unsaved religious people in various denominations and religions. Such people claim to believe in God, but don't know Him as a true child of God with salvation. The Bible was written to make us wise unto salvation through faith in Christ Jesus (2 Tim. 3:15).

While it might seem to make perfect sense in the natural that we can pass our love and worship on to the one represented by a statue, this is not the way God has chosen for us to do these things. Bowing before and kissing an image is condemned by Scripture as idolatry. Furthermore, such actually is an expression of hatred towards God (Ex. 20:4,5) even though it is done unknowingly. God wants us to worship him in spirit and in truth (John 4:23). Scripture declares we show our love for Jesus and God by *obeying* their commands (John 14:15; 1 John 5:3).

It is somewhat common for Catholics to think a person who left the Catholic religion has joined a *cult* or some false religion. Perhaps at times, this is a clever design to stop others who know that person from considering their Scriptural arguments. Certainly for the ones who find salvation through reading the Bible and placing their faith in Jesus, such a departure from Catholicism is based on truth and fear of God, as defined in Scripture.

It is out of love for the person that former Catholics who

are now Christians share the truths that were spoken to Maria. If her sister hated her she wouldn't say anything and just let her continue in these false ways which will end in spiritual disaster. To label such a concerned Christian a *Catholic basher,* or the like, is nothing but a slanderous, untrue charge. All people, regardless if they are Catholic or not, vitally need to know the truth about salvation. It is the Christian's responsibility before God to spread these Scriptural truths to every person, regardless what denomination they are in. Such truth can seem very disturbing for those who are embracing falsehood and desire to remain there.

The Catholic Church teaches that Mary is the "Gate" between Heaven and Earth and ascribes many other unscriptural titles and concepts to her. Another very common one is that she is "our life, sweetness and hope," as expressed in the Rosary. Such is not the Mary of the Bible, but a horrible and dangerous distortion of the truth about the mother of Jesus of Nazareth. In contrast to all of these Catholic concepts about Mary being connected with our salvation, we have the word of God which states such belongs uniquely to the Lord Jesus. The object of our faith is clearly shown, in the New Testament, to be the *one* who died on the cross for our sins and rose again from the grave. He is the *one* who was preached about by the apostles, for salvation is only found in Jesus (Acts 4:12).

Concisely stated, these are the facts that God wants all people to know: We must get Biblically saved and then stay saved to enter his paradise kingdom after physical death. Sadly though, staying saved doesn't always happen. Many people truly turn from their sins and submit their will to the Lord Jesus as they trust him for salvation, but afterwards they depart from the faith and go back to their old sins. Such apostates (former Christians) need to know that there will be no entrance into God's kingdom for them apart from following Jesus and remaining faithful to him to the end. They must again repent and come back to God (as the prodigal did) to become *alive again* (Luke 15:24, 32). To

be saved (that is, actually enter God's paradise, eternal kingdom), a true disciple must endure the hatred that will come for
following Jesus to the end of his life (Mt. 10:22; Heb. 3:14). All
of these truths and much more are found in the New Testament.
What one does with the message of the Bible will indeed affect
his eternal destiny. This includes YOU, the reader. God bless
you. For more information, please come to our web site at www.
evangelicaloutreach.org You may also contact us by mail at:
Evangelical Outreach, PO Box 265, Washington, PA 15301.♥

Appendix A: Marian Feasts

The 16 most common Feast Days of the *Mary of Catholicism* are:

January 1 - Solemnity of Mary
January 8 - Our Lady of Prompt Succor
February 2 - Presentation of the Lord
February 11- Our Lady of Lourdes
March 25 - Annunciation
May 31 - Visitation
June 27 - Our Mother of Perpetual Help
July 16 - Our Lady of Mount Carmel
August 15 - Assumption
August 22 - Queenship of Mary
September 8 - Birth of Mary
September 15 - Our Lady of Sorrows
October 7 - Our Lady of the Rosary
November 21 - Presentation of the Blessed Virgin Mary
December 8 - Immaculate Conception
December 12 - Our Lady of Guadalupe

A much more exhaustive list of Marian feasts is below. **You will notice that whole months are set aside for Mary devotion. May is Mary month, but August, September and October are also especially important for Mary devotees.**

JANUARY
MONTH of the HOLY NAME

1. Solemnity of Mary Mother of God
2. Foundation of the Abbey of Dunes, Flanders, in honor of the Blessed Virgin

3. Our Lady of Sichem, Belgium
4. Our Lady of Treves, Italy
5. Our Lady of Abundance or Prosperity, Cursi, Italy
6. Our Lady of Cana
7. Our Lady of Egypt
8. Our Lady of Prompt Succor, New Orleans, Louisiana
9. Our Lady of Beyond the Tiber, Rome, Our Lady of Clemency, or Mercy of Absam,
    near Innsbruck, Austria
10. Our Lady of the Guides, Constantinople
11. Our Lady of Bessiere, Limousin, France
12. Our Lady of the Broad Street, Rome
13. Our Lady of Victory, Prague, Czechosolovakia
14. Our Lady of the Word, Montserrat, Spain
15. Our Lady of the Crops, Syria
    Our Lady of Banneux, Belgium
16. Our Lady, Refuge of sinners.
    Our Lady of Montserrat delivers captives from tyranny of Turks, Spain
17. Our Lady of Peace, Rome
18. Our Lady of Dijon, France
19. Our Lady of Gimout, Citeaux, France
20. Our Lady of Tables, Montpellier, France. "Arms of the city of Montpellier"
21. Our Lady of Consolation, Rome
22. Eve of Our Lady's Espousals to St. Joseph
23. Feast of Our Lady's Espousals
24. Our Lady of Damascus
25. Translation of the winding sheet and tomb of Our Lady to Constantinople
26. Our Lady of Long Fields, Madrid, Spain
27. Our Lady of Life, Provence, France
28. Our Lady of Good Succor, near Rouen, France
29. Our Lady of Chatillon sur Seine, France. Appeared to St. Bernard
30. Our Lady of the Rose, Lucca, Italy
31. Apparition of Our Lady to Bl. Angela de Foligny

FEBRUARY
MONTH of the PASSION of OUR LORD

1. Eve of the Purification of Our Lady
2. Purification of Our Lady
3. Our Lady of Saideneida, Damascus
4. Our Lady of Fire, Forli, Italy
5. Dedication of the First Church of Our Lady by St. Peter in Tortosa, Italy
6. Our Lady of Louvain, Belgium
7. Our Lady of Grace
8. Abbey of Our Lady of the Lily, Melun, France
9. Our Lady of the Bells
10. Our Lady of the Dove, Bologna, Italy
11. Our Lady of Lourdes, France
12. Our Lady of Argenteuil, Paris
13. Our Lady of Pellevoisin, France
14. Our Lady of Bourbourg, Flanders
15. Our Lady of Paris, France

16. Our Lady of the Thorn, Chalons-sur-Marne, France
17. Our Lady of Constantinople, Bari, Turkey
18. Our Lady of Laon, Rheims, France
19. Our Lady of Good Tidings, Lempdes, France
20. Our Lady of Bolougne sur Mer, France
21. Our Lady of Bon Port, Dol
22. Our Lady of Succour, Rennes, France
23. Our Lady of Rocks, near Salamanca, Spain
24. Plague in Rome ends after Pope St. Gregory the Great leads procession with a
    painting by St Luke of Our Lady
25. Our Lady of Victory, Constantinople
26. Our Lady of the Fields, Paris France
27. Our Lady of Light, Lisbon, Portugal and Palermo, Italy
28. Institution of the Monastery of the Annunciation, Bethune, France

MARCH
MONTH of ST. JOSEPH

1. Our Lady Della Croce, Crema, Italy
2. Our Lady of Apparitions, Madrid, Spain
3. Our Lady of Angels of Toulouse, France
       Our Lady of Longport, Valois, France
4. Our Lady de la Guard, Marseille, France
5. Our Lady of Good Help, Montreal Canada
6. Our Lady of Nazareth, Pierre Noire, Portugal
7. Our Lady of the Star, Villa Viciosa, Portugal
8. Our Lady of Virtues, Lisbon, Portugal.
9. Our Lady of Savigny, France
10. Our Lady of the Vine, Tuscany, Italy
11. Our Lady of the Forests, Porto, Portugal
12. Our Lady of Miracles, St. Maur des Fosses, France
13. Our Lady of the Empress, Rome
14. Our Lady de la Breche, Chartres, France
15. Our Lady of the Underground, Chartres, France
16. Our Lady of the Fountain, Constantinople
17. Our Lady of Ireland or the Madonna of Ireland
       Office of Our Lady Instituted, Pope Urban II
18. Cathedral of Our Lady of Loretto
19. The Beautiful Lady, Nogent-sur-Seine, France
20. Our Lady of Calevourt, near Brussels, Belgium
21. Our Lady of Bruges, Flanders
22. Our Lady of Citeaux, France
23. Our Lady of Victory of Lepanto, Hungary
24. Eve of the Annunciation, instituted by Gregory II
25. Solemnity of the Annunciation of the Lord to Our Lady, instituted by the apostles, and
       the most ancient of all feasts
26. Our Lady of Soissons, France
27. Apparition of Our Lord to Our Lady, as soon as He was risen from the dead
28. Our Lady of Castelbruedo, Catalonia, Spain
29. Apparation of Our Lady
30. Re-establishment of the chapel of Our Lady

31. Our Lady of the Holy Cross, Jerusalem

*Passion Sunday - The Seven Dolors of Our Lady (traditional)

APRIL
MONTH of the HOLY EUCHARIST

1. Our Lady of Tears
2. Our Lady of the Highest Grace, Higuey, Dominican Republic
3. Apparition of Our Lord to Our Lady & the Apostles in the upper room
4. Our Lady of Grace, Normandy, France
5. Apparition of Our Lady to Pope Honorius IV in Confirmation of the Order of Our Lady of Mount Carmel
6. Our Lady of the Conception, Flanders
7. Our Lady of Puig, Valencia, Spain
8. Our Lady of the Valley, Sicily
9. Our Lady of Myans, Savoy, France
10. Our Lady of Laval
11. Our Lady of Fourviere, France
12. Our Lady of Charity, Cobre, Cuba
13. Apparation of Our Lady to Bl. Jane of Mantua
14. Apparition of Our Lady to St. Ludwina
15. Our Lady of Keiff, Russia
16. Our Lady of Victories in the Church of St. Mark, Venice
17. Our Lady of Arabida, Portugal
18. Pope Urban VI grants plenary indulgence to those who visit the Church of Our Lady of Loretto
19. Our Lady of Lyons, France
20. Our Lady of Schier, Bavaria
21. Institution of the Confraternity of the Immaculate Conception, Toledo, Spain
22. Our Lady of Betharam, France
23. Pope Calixtus III grants indulgences to those who visit the Cathedral of Arras, where a veil and cinture of Our Lady is kept
24. Our Lady of Bonaria, Island of Sardinia
25. Dedication of the Lower Holy Chapel of Paris in honor of Our Lady
26. Our Lady of Good Counsel
27. Our Lady La Moreneta, Spain
28. Our Lady of the Oak, Anjou, France
29. Our Lady of Faith, Amiens, France
30. Our Lady of Africa, Algiers

*Saturday after Ascension—Our Lady, Queen of Apostles

MAY
MONTH of OUR LADY

1. Our Lady Queen of the May
2. Our Lady of Oviedo, Spain
3. Our Lady of Jasna Gora, Poland
4. Our Lady the Helper, Normandy, France
5. Our Lady Queen of the Apostles

6. Our Lady of Miracles in the Church of Our Lady of Peace, Rome
7. Our Lady of Haut, in Hainault
8. Our Lady of Pompeii
9. Our Lady of Loretto, Ancona, Italy
10. Dedication of Constantinople to Our Lady by Constantine the Great
11. Our Lady of Aparecida, Patroness of Brazil
12. Our Lady of Power, Aubervillers, France
13. Dedication of Our Lady of Martyrs, Rome
14. Our Lady of Bavaria
15. Our Lady of France
16. Apparition of Our Lady to St. Catherine of Alexandria
17. Our Lady of Tears, Spoletto, Italy
18. Dedication of Our Lady of Bonport Abbey, Diocese of Evreux
19. Our Lady of Flines, Douay
20. Dedication of the Church of La Ferté, Burgundy, in honor of Our Lady
21. Our Lady of Vladmir, Russia
22. Our Lady of Monte Vergine, near Naples, Italy
23. Our Lady of Miracles of Brescia, Italy
24. Our Lady Help of Christians, Europe
25. Our Lady of the New Jerusalem
26. Our Lady of Caravaggio, Italy
27. Our Lady of Naples, Italy
28. Feast of the Relics of Our Lady, Venice, Italy
29. Our Lady of Ardents, Arras, France
30. Our Lady of the Sacred Heart, Mexico
31. Feast of the Visitation

*Last Saturday of the Month of May - Our Lady of the Sacred Heart

JUNE
MONTH of the SACRED HEART

1. Our Lady of the Star, Aquileia, Italy
2. Our Lady of Edessa, Asia Minor in honor of the statue that spoke to St. Alexis
3. Our Lady of Sasopoli, Italy
4. Our Lady of the Hill, Lombardy, Italy
5. Our Lady of Haut, Hainault, France
6. Institution of the Nuns of the Visitation of Our Lady, by St Francis de Sales
7. Our Lady of Marienthal, Germany
8. Our Lady of Alexandria, Egypt
9. Our Lady of Mentorello, Italy
10. Our Lady of Cranganor, India
11. Our Lady of Esquernes, Flanders
12. Apparition of Our Lady to St. Herman, France
13. Dedication of the Church of Our Lady of Sichem, Belgium
14. Our Lady of Arras, France
15. Foundation of Our Lady of the Feuillants, Toulouse, France
16. Our Lady of Aix la Chapelle, Germany
17. Our Lady of the Forest, Britanny, France
18. Appearance of Our Lady to St. Agnes of Monte Pulciano, Italy
19. Our Lady of Monte Senario, Florence, Italy

20. Our Lady of Consolation, Luxemburg
21. Our Lady of Matarieh, at Grand Cairo, Egypt
22. Our Lady of Narni, Italy
23. Our Lady Justinienne at Carthage
24. Our Lady of Clos Evrard, Trier, Germany
25. Divine Motherhood of Our Lady, declared at the Council of Ephesus
26. Our Lady of Meliapore, East Indies
27. Our Lady of Perpetual Help
28. Institution of the Angelus of Our Lady, Europe
29. Our Lady of Buglose, France
30. Our Lady of Calais, France

*Saturday following the second Sunday after Pentecost—The Feast of the Immaculate Heart of Mary

JULY
MONTH of the MOST PRECIOUS BLOOD

1. Dedication of the Church of Jumieges, Normandy, France
2. Feast of the Visitation of Our Lady
3. Our Lady of la Carolle, Paris
4. Our Lady of Miracles, Avignon, France
5. Dedication of Our Lady of Cambray, Arras, France
6. Our Lady D'Iron, Dunois, France
7. Our Lady of Arras, Netherlands
8. Our Lady of Kazan, Russia
9. Our Lady of the Atonment, Graymoor, New York
10. Our Lady of Boulogne, France
11. Our Lady of Clery, near Orleans, France
12. Our Lady of Lure, Avignon, France
13. Image of Our Lady of Chartres, France
14. Our Lady of the Bush, Portugal
15. Our Lady of Molanus, Jerusalem
16. Our Lady of Mt. Carmel, Feast of the Brown Scapular
17. Our Lady of Campitelli, Italy
18. Our Lady of Victory at Toledo, Spain
19. Our Lady of Moyen Point, near Peronne, France
20. Our Lady of Grace, at Picpus, Faubourg Saint Antoine, of Paris
21. Our Lady of Verdun, Lorraine
22. Our Lady of Safety or of Safe Hiding, Overloon, Holland
23. Institution of the Order of Our Lady of Premontre, Lancaster, England
24. Foundation of Our Lady of Cambron, France
25. Our Lady of Lac Bouchet, Quebec
26. Our Lady of Faith, Cauchy
27. Our Lady of Faith, Gravelines
28. Victory over the Turks by the Knights of Rhodes in 1480 through Our Lady's intercession
29. Our Lady of Deliverance, Madrid, Spain
30. Our Lady de Gray, France
31. Our Lady of the Slain, Lorban, Portugal

*Saturday before the fourth Sunday of July—Mother of Mercy

AUGUST
MONTH of the IMMACULATE HEART of MARY

1. Our Lady Asks for Establishment of an Order for Redeeming Captives
2. Our Lady of Angels, Assisi, Italy
3. Our Lady of Bows, London
4. Our Lady of Dordrecht, Holland
5. Our Lady of the Snows Rome, Italy
6. Our Lady of Capacabana, Bolivia
7. Our Lady of Schiedam, Holland
8. Our Lady of Kuehn, near Brussels, Belgium
9. Our Lady of Oegnies, Brabant, Netherlands
10. Institution of the Order of Our Lady of Mercy, Barcelona, Spain
11. Emperor Charlemagne Receives 2 of the Blessed Virgin's Robes from Emperor Nicephorus and Empress Irene
12. Our Lady of Rouen, France
13. Dormition of Our Lady
14. Vigil of the Assumption of Our Lady
15. Solemnity of the Assumption of the Blessed Virgin Mary into Heaven (Instituted by Pope Leo IV in 847)
16. Our Lady of Trapani, Sicily
17. Victory of the King of France (Philip the Fair), imploring the Help of Our Lady of Chartres
18. Coronation of Our Lady
19. Our Lady of the Don, Russia
20. Our Lady of St. Bernard's "Ave," Brabant, Netherlands
21. Our Lady of Knock, Ireland
22. Queenship of Mary - Octave of the Assumption
23. Our Lady of Victory of Valois, France
24. Our Lady, Health of the Sick
25. Our Lady of Rossano, Calabria, Italy
26. Our Lady of Czestochowa, Poland
27. Our Lady of Moustier, France
28. Our Lady of Kiev, Russia
29. Our Lady of Clermont, Poland
30. Our Lady of Carquere, Portugal
31. Our Lady of the Founders, Constantinople

*Saturday before the last Sunday of August—Our Lady, Health of the Sick
*Saturday after the Feast of St. Augustine (Aug. 28)—Our Lady of Consolation

SEPTEMBER
MONTH of OUR LADY of SORROWS

1. Collection of all the Feasts of Our Lady, celebrated at Louvain
2. Our Lady of Helbron, Germany
3. Our Lady of the Divine Shepherd, France
4. Our Lady of Haut, Restores Life to Young Woman, Belgium
5. Our Lady of the Woods, Galloro

6. Our Lady of the Fountain, Valenciennes, France
7. Vigil of the Nativity of Our Lady, instituted by Pope Gregory II
8. The Nativity of the Blessed Virgin Mary
9. Our Lady of Le Puy, France
10. Our Lady of Trut, the Shrine near Cologne, Germany, built by St. Heribert
11. Our Lady of Hildesheim, Germany
12. The Holy Name of Mary
13. Our Lady of Zell (Mariazell), Austria
14. Our Lady of Einsiedeln, Switzerland
15. Feast of the 7 Sorrows of Mary
16. Our Lady of Good News, Sicily
17. Our Lady of the Candles
18. Our Lady of Smelcem, Flanders
19. Our Lady of La Salette, France
20. Our Lady of the Silver Foot, at Toul in Lorraine, France
21. Our Lady of Pucha, Valentia
22. The Giving of the Name of Mary to Our Lady by St. Ann, Her mother
23. Our Lady of Valvenere, Spain
24. Our Lady of Ransom, Spain
25. Madonna, Divine Shepherdess, Spain
26. Our Lady of Victory at Tourney
27. Our Lady of Happy Assemby, Le Laus, France
28. Our Lady of Cambron, France
29. Our Lady of Tongres, France
30. Our Lady of Beaumont, Lorraine, France

OCTOBER
MONTH of the HOLY ROSARY

1. Foundation of the Abbey de la Couronne in Angouleme
2. Our Lady of the Assumption, Naples, Italy
3. Our Lady of the Place, Rome
4. Our Lady of Vaussivieres, Auvergne, France
5. Our Lady of Buch, Guienne
6. Our Lady of All Help
7. Feast of the Rosary, instituted by Pope Gregory XIII
8. Church of Our Lady of Gifts, Avignon, France
9. Miraculous Cure of St. John Damascene by Our Lady
10. Our Lady of the Cloister, Citeaux, France
11. Feast of the Divine Maternity of Our Lady
12. Our Lady of the Pillar, Saragossa, Spain
13. Our Lady of Clairveaux, France
14. Our Lady of Larochelle, France
15. Dedication of the Church of Our Lady of Terouenne
16. Dedication of the Church of Our Lady of Milan
17. Dedication of the Cave of Our Lady of Chartres, France
18. Dedication of the Church of Our Lady of Rheims
19. Dedication of Holy Cross and Our Lady Abbey, Royaumont, France
20. Dedication of the Abbey of Our Lady, Pontigny, France
21. Our Lady of Talan, near Dijon, France
22. Our Lady of the Under-ground, Grand Cairo

23. Our Lady of Consolation, near Honfleur, France
24. Our Lady of Hermits, Switzerland
25. Dedication of the Cathedral of Our Lady of Toledo, Spain
26. Our Lady of Victory, near Senlis, France
27. Dedication of the Basilica of Our Lady, Help of Christians, Turin, Italy
28. Our Lady of Vivonne, Savoy, France
29. Our Lady of Oropa, Vercelli, Italy
30. Our Lady of Mondevi, Piedmont
31. Miracle at St. Fort, Chartres, France

NOVEMBER
MONTH of the HOLY SOULS

1. Our Lady of the Palm, Cadiz, Spain
2. Our Lady of Emminont, Abbeville, France
3. Our Lady of Rennes, Britianny, France
4. Our Lady of Port Louis, Milan, Italy
5. Our Lady of Damietta, Egypt
6. Our Lady of Valfleurie, Lyons, France
7. Our Lady of the Pond, Dijon, France
8. Our Lady of Belle Fontaine, La Rochelle
9. Our Lady of Almudena, Madrid, Spain
10. Miraculous cure through the intercession of Our Lady of Loretto
11. Our Lady of the Portuguese
12. Our Lady of the Tower Secret, Turin, Italy
13. Our Lady of Nanteuil, France
14. Our Lady of the Grotto, Lamego, Portugal
15. Our Lady of Pignerol, Savoy, France
16. Our Lady of Chieves, Hainault, Belgium
17. Our Lady of Sion (Queen of the Jews)
18. The Rosary Virgin of Chiquinquira, Columbia
19. Our Lady of Good News or Glad Tidings
20. Our Lady of La Guarde, Bologna, Italy
21. Presentation of the Blessed Virgin Mary
22. Our Lady of Lavang, Viet Nam
23. Our Lady of the Vault, Italy
24. Our Lady of Montserrat, Spain
25. Our Lady of the Rock of Fiesola, Tuscany, Italy
26. Our Lady of the Mountains, Italy
27. Our Lady of the Miraculous Medal
28. Our Lady of Walsingham, England
29. Apparition of Our Lady of Beauraing, Belgium
30. Our Lady of Genesta, Genoa, Italy

*Saturday before the third Sunday of November—Mary, Mother of Divine Providence

DECEMBER
MONTH of the DIVINE INFANCY

1. Our Lady of Ratisbon, Bavaria
2. Our Lady of Didinia, Cappadocia, Turkey

3. Our Lady of Filermo, Malta
4. Our Lady of La Chapelle, Abbeville
5. Our Lady of the Jesuits College, Rome
6. Our Lady of Seez, built by St. Latuin
7. Our Lady of Paris
8. Solemnity of the Immaculate Conception of the Blessed Virgin Mary
9. Our Lady of the Conception, Naples, Italy
10. Transition of the Holy House of Loretto, Italy
11. Our Lady of Angels, Paris
12. Our Lady of Guadalupe, Patroness of the Americas, Mexico
13. Our Lady of the Holy Chapel, Paris
14. Our Lady of Alba Royale, Hungary
15. Our Lady of the Armed Forces
16. Our Lady of Good or Happy Deliverance
17. Our Lady of Amiens, France
18. The Expectation of Our Lady
19. Our Lady of Toledo, Spain
20. Our Lady of Molene, France
21. Our Lady of St. Acheul, Amiens, France
22. Our Lady of Chartres, Mother of Youth, France
23. Our Lady of Ardilliers, Anjou, France
24. Chaste Nuptials of Our Lady and St. Joseph
25. Birth of Jesus Christ, Lord and God
26. Our Lady of Acheropita, Rossano, Italy
27. Institution of the Knights of Our Lady
28. Our Lady of Pontoise, France
29. Our Lady of Spire, Germany
30. Our Lady of Bologna, Italy
31. Image of Our Lady of Chartres brings back to life the son of King Geoffry

*Our Lady of All Nations ?

Appendix B: More Titles For Mary

Pope John Paul II comments on the *many titles* given to the *Mary of Catholicism*:

> As the **many titles** attributed to the Blessed Virgin and the continual pilgrimages to Marian shrines attest, the **trust of the faithful in Jesus' Mother** spurs them **to call upon her** for their daily needs.[1]

John Paul II did not hint at just how many *titles* are attributed to Mary. In this appendix, you will see two listings of various titles given to Mary. The first contains some of the most common titles while the second are less common. Please be assured that even the lengthy second listing is not exhaustive:

Adam's Deliverance; Advocate of Eve; Advocate of Sinners; All Chaste; All Fair and Immaculate; All Good; Annunciation of the Blessed Virgin; Aqueduct of Grace; Archetype fo Purity and Innocence; Ark Gilded by the Holy Spirit; Ark of the Covenant Assumption of the Blessed Virgin; Basillica of Saint Mary Major; Blessed Among Women; Blessed Virgin Mary; Bridal Chamber of the Lord; Bride of Christ; Bride of Heaven; Bride of the Canticle; Bride of the Father; Bride Unbrided; Cause of Our Joy; Chosen Before the Ages; Comfort of Christians; Comforter of the Afflicted; Conceived Without Original Sin; Consoler of the Afflicted; Co-Redemptrix; Court of the Eternal King; Created Temple of the Creator; Crown of Virginity; Daughter of Men; David's Daughter; Deliverer From All Wrath; Deliverer of Christian Nations; Destroyer of Heresies; Dispenser of Grace; Dwelling Place for God;

---

1   *Theotókos*, p. 257.

Dwelling Place Meet for God; Dwelling Place of the Illimitable; Dwelling Place of the Spirit; Earth Unsown; Earth Untouched and Virginal; Eastern Gate; Ever Green and Fruitful; Ever Virgin; Eve's Tears Redeeming; Exalted Above the Angels; Feast of the Immaculate Conception; Fleece of Heavenly Rain; Flower of Jesse's Root; Formed Without Sin; Forthbringer of God; Forthbringer of the Ancient of Days; Forthbringer of the Tree of Life; Fountain of Living Water; Fountain Sealed; Free From Every Stain; Full of Grace; Garden Enclosed; Gate of Heaven; God's Eden; God's Olive Tree; God's Vessel; Handmaid of the Lord; Healing Balm of Integrity; Health of the Sick; Helper of All in Danger; Holy in Soul and Body; Holy Mountain of Our Lady; Hope of Christians; House Built by Wisdom; House of Gold; Immaculate; Immaculate Conception; Immaculate Heart; Immaculate Heart of Mary; Immaculate Mary; Immaculate Mother; Immaculate Virgin; Incorruptible Wood of the Ark; Inventrix of Grace; Inviolate; Joseph's Spouse; Kingly Throne; King's Mother; Lady Most Chaste; Lady Most Venerable; Lady of Good Help; Lady of Grace; Lady of Mercy; Lady of Peace; Lady of Perpetual Help; Lady of the Rosary; Lady of Sorrows; Lady of Victory; Lamp Unquenchable; Life-Giver to Posterity; Light Cloud of Heavenly Rain; Lily Among Thorns; Living Temple of the Deity; Loom of the Incarnation; Madonna; Madonna of Saint Luke; Marketplace for Salutary Exchange; Mary of the Hurons; Mary the Blessed Virgin; Mary; Blessed Virgin; Mary; Help of Christians; Mary; Mother of God; Mary; Queen of Africa; Mary; Queen of Angels; Mary; Queen of Peace; Mary; Star of the Sea; Mediatrix; Mediatrix and Conciliatrix; Mediatrix of All Graces; Mediatrix of Salvation; Mediatrix of the Mediator; Minister of Life; Mirror of Justice; More Beautiful Than Beauty; More Glorious Than Paradise More Gracious Than Grace; More Holy Than the Cherubim, the Seraphim and the Entire Angelic Hosts; Morning Star; Most Venerable; Mother and Virgin; Mother Most Admirable; Mother Most Amiable; Mother Most Chaste; Mother Most Pure; Mother Inviolate; Mother of Christians; Mother of Christ's Members; Mother of Divine Grace; Mother of God; Mother of Good Counsel; Mother of Jesus Christ; Mother of Men; Mother of Our Creator; Mother of Our Head; Mother of Our Savior; Mother of the Church; Mother of the Mystical Body; Mother of Wisdom; Mother Undefiled; My Body's Healing; My Soul's Saving; Mystical Rose; Nativity of the Blessed Virgin; Nature's Re-Creation; Nature's Restoration; Neck of the Mystical Body; Never Fading Wood; New Eve; Notre Dame Cathedral of Paris; Notre Dame of Chartres; Notre Dame of Easton; Nourisher of God and Man; Olive Tree of the Father's Compassion; Only Bridge of God to Men; Our Immaculate Queen; Our Lady; Gate of Heaven; Our Lady; Help of Christians; Our Lady; Mother of the Church; Our Lady; Queen of All Saints; Our Lady; Queen of the Apostles; Our Lady in America; Our Lady Mediatrix of All Grace; Our Lady of Africa; Our Lady of Altotting; Our Lady of Bandel; Our Lady of Bandra; Our Lady of Banneux; Our Lady of Baeuraing; Our Lady of Calvary; Our Lady of Charity; Our Lady of Consolation; Our Lady of Copacabana; Our Lady of Czestochowa; Our Lady of Europe; Our Lady of Fatima; Our Lady of Good Council; Our Lady of Good Help; Our Lady of Good Remedy; Our Lady of Grace; Our Lady of Guadalupe; Our Lady of Guadalupe of Estramadura; Our Lady of High Grace; Our Lady of Hungary; Our Lady of Japan; Our Lady of Kevelaer; Our Lady of Knock; Our Lady of La Leche; Our Lady of La Vang; Our Lady of Las Vegas; Our Lady of LaSallette; Our Lady of Limerick; Our Lady of Loreto; Our Lady of Lourdes; Our Lady of Lujan; Our Lady of Madhu; Our Lady of Mariazell; Our Lady of Medjugore; Our Lady of Mercy; Our Lady of Montserrat; Our Lady of Mount Carmel; Our Lady of Mount Carmel at Aylesford; Our Lady of Nazareth; Our Lady of Peace; Our Lady of Perpetual Help; Our Lady of Pompeii Our Lady of Pontmain; Our Lady of Prompt Succor; Our Lady of Providence; Our Lady of Ransom; Our Lady of Safe Travel; Our Lady of Salambao; Our Lady of Shongweni; Our Lady of Sorrows; Our Lady of Tears; Our Lady of Victory; Our Lady of Walsingham; Our Lady of the Americas; Our Lady of the Assumption; Our Lady of the Cape; Our Lady of the Gulf; Our Lady of the Hermits; Our Lady of the Highways; Our Lady of the Holy Rosary; Our Lady of the Holy Souls; Our Lady of the Immaculate

Conception; Our Lady of the Incarnation; Our Lady of the Kodiak and the Islands; Our Lady of the Milk and Happy Delivery; Our Lady of the Miraculous Medal; Our Lady of the Pillar of Saragossa; Our Lady of the Pines; Our Lady of the Prairie; Our Lady of the Presentation; Our Lady of the Rosary; Our Lady of the Scapular; Our Lady of the Snows; Our Lady of the Turumba; Our Lady of the Valley; Our Lady of the Wayside; Our Lady of the Woods; Our Lady Who Appeared; Our Own Sweet Mother; Paradise Fenced Against the Serpent; Paradise of Innocence and Immortality; Paradise of the Second Adam; Paradise Planted by God; Patroness and Protectoress; Perfume of Faith; Preserved From All Sin; Protectress From All Hurt; Queen of All Saints; Queen of Angels; Queen of Creation; Queen of Heaven; Queen of Heaven and Earth; Queen of Martyrs; Queen of Peace; Queen Unconquered; Refuge in Time of Danger; Refuge of Sinners; Reparatrix; Reparatrix of Her Parents; Reparatrix of the Lord World; Rich in Mercy Rose Ever Blooming; Sacred Heart of Mary; Sanctuary of the Holy Spirit; Scepter of Orthodoxy; Seat of Wisdom; Second Eve; Singular Vessel of Devotion; Sister and Mother; Source of Virginity; Spiritual Vessel; Spotless Dove of Beauty; Star of the Sea; Star That Bore the Sea; Suppliant for Sinners; Surpassing Eden's Gardens; Surpassing the Heavens; Surpassing the Seraphim; Sweet Flowering and Gracious Mercy; Tabernacle of God; Tabernacle of the Word; Temple Divine; Temple Indestructible; Temple of the Lord's Body; Theotokos; Throne of the King; Tower of David; Tower of Ivory; Tower Unassailable; Treasure House of Life Treasure of Immortality; Treasure of the World Undefiled; Undefiled Treasure of Virginity; Undug Well of Remission's Waters; Unlearned in the Ways of Eve; Unplowed Field of Heaven's Bread; Unwatered Vineyard of Immortality's Wine; Vessel of Honor; Victor Over the Serpent; Virgin Inviolate; Virgin Most Faithful; Virgin Most Merciful; Virgin Most Powerful; Virgin Most Prudent; Virgin Most Pure; Virgin Mother; Virgin of Charity; Virgin of Copacabana; Virgin of Virgins; Wedded to God; Woman Clothed With the Sun; and Workshop of the Incarnation.

The *Mary of Catholicism's* Less Common Titles

Beautiful as the sun; Beautiful surpassingly;Beloved daughter;Beloved of God; Beloved spouse of the Spirit of God; Blessed among women;Blessed Mary ever a virgin;Blessed from generation to generation; Blessed one;Blessed root of glory; Bride of heaven; Bride of the blessed Trinity; Bride of the Holy Ghost; Bride of the Spirit with his sevenfold gifts; Bright as the sun; Brightest glory of the human race;Called blessed by all generations; Celestial glories round thee blaze; Charity without measure; Cherished spouse of the Holy Ghost;Chief support of the primitive Church; Chosen from the ages; Chosen spouse of the Holy Spirit; Coadjutrix in the work of human redemption; Compared with thee, the Powers are weakness; Conflagration of love; Constancy without parallel; Co-Redemptrix; Daughter of God the Father; Daughter of King David; Daughter of the Eternal Father; Delight of the Holy Trinity; Descendant of kings, patriarchs and prophets; Desired of all nations; Divine prodigy; Elect and predestined from all eternity; Endowed with all perfections and the whole range of infused virtues; Ever glorious and blessed Mary; Every manner of honor, of grace, of merit and of glory is found in Mary; Exalted above all the choirs of angels and orders of saints; Exalted above all things save only God himself; Exalted by divine grace above all angels and men; Exalted by God above all the choirs of angels; Exalted in heaven above every living creature; Expected by the patriarchs; Fair daughter; Fair spouse of Jehovah, whose Son is thy child; Fairest amongst all the daughters of Jerusalem; Fairest among women; Fairest thou where all are fair; Faithful handmaid; Faithful to grace in the highest degree; Favorite daughter of the Father; First of all God's creatures in heaven; Flower of God's choosing, that shall never fade; Forth-bringer of God; Full of grace; Full of the Holy Ghost; Gentlest of the gentle; Glorious and perpetual virgin Mary; Glorious mother of God; Glory of angels; Glory of God; Glory of our race; Glory of the Christian people; Glory of the priesthood; Glory of the works of the Almighty; God's garden of delights; God has chosen and pre-elected her, and has made her to dwell in his tabernacle; God's masterpiece; Great lady at the right hand of her Divine Son; Great princess; Greatest and most sublime of all creatures; Greatest work of the Divine Majesty; Hail Mary full of grace; Handmaid of the Lord; Heavenly Phoenix; Heavenly princess; Heir of a royal line which goes back to Joachim, to Solomon, to David, to Jesse, to Abraham, to Adam; Herald of Jesus; Higher than the angels; His companion for all eternity, possessing such a likeness to Him, that none greater can be possible between a God-man and a creature; Holy, holy, holy Mary; Honor, glory and firmament of our Church; Honored with the glory of maternity; Humble because she was all for God; In Mary all created perfections, but in a most excellent manner and degree; In thy conception, O virgin Mary, thou wast immaculate; Incomparably greater than all other creatures; Jesus is omnipotent of himself; Mary is all powerful through her Son; Joseph's spouse; Joy of paradise; Joy of the blest; Joy of the universal Church; Light of the faithful; Lily of spotless whiteness; Loveliest whom in heaven they see; More beautiful than the sun; More fair than morn's refulgent rays that flame in eastern majesty; More glorious than the Cherubim; More glorious than the supernal spirits; More honorable than the Seraphim; Most glorious virgin Mary; Most perfect woman; Most pure and holy of all creatures; Mother and spouse of God; Mother of the Eternal Son; Mother of the only begotten Son of the Eternal Father; New Eve; Noble daughter, most beloved of our common Lord; O wonder, who, after all wonders, art still the most wonderful; Omnipotent in prayer; Omnipotent through grace; Paradise of delights; Paradise of God; Partaker of perpetual benediction; Patroness of graces; Peerless and singular creature; Perfect beatitude; Powerful vanquisher of all heresies; Prepared for himself by the Most High; Preserved from the inherited guilt of original sin; Purest, holiest, fairest of creatures; Purest humanity; Ravisher of hearts; Reparatrix; Rose of all roses; Sagacious woman; Saint of saints; Seat of all divine graces; Seat of wisdom; Servant of the Spirit; She by herself is more like to her Son than all the saints together; She obtains a splendor and eminence surpassing the excellence of all created things; Singular and chosen creature; So lowly in thine own eyes, but so great in the eyes of the Lord; Sovereign of angels; Splendor of all heaven; Spouse and temple of the Holy Ghost; Spouse of the Blessed Trinity; Spouse of the Canticle of Canticles; Spouse of the divine Spirit; Spouse of the Holy Ghost; Spouse of the Most High; Supereffulgent star; Sweeter than honey; The all-holy one; The chosen one, who is to be acceptable above all creatures; The crown and joy of all of the saints; The daughters of Sion beheld her and declared her most blessed and queens have praised her; The desired of nations; The exaltation of humanity; The fairest of all creatures; The fruit of benediction; The glories of Mary for the sake of her Son; The glory of Jerusalem; The glory of paradise; The great honor of our people; The greatest of women and none can compare; The Holy One who will be born of thee shall be called the Son of God; The honor of our race; The honor of the martyrs; The honor of us all; The immaculate virgin mother of God, after completing her earthly course, was assumed body and soul into heavenly glory; The joy of Israel; The joy of our country; The most illustrious glory and ornament, and most firm guardian of the Holy Church; The one blessed beyond all others; The one without the slightest stain; The praise of the prophets and apostles; The sacred Spirit's fruitful spouse; The Spirit's chosen spouse; The true and only spouse of the Holy Spirit; The victor in all the battles of God; The virgin Mary is taken up to the heavenly chamber, in which the King of Kings sits upon his starry throne; There is an infinite difference between God's servants and His mother; Thou art blessed and venerable; Thou hast begotten life and glory for all generations of men; Thou has far excelled every other work of God; Thou hast found grace with the Lord; Thou lookest down on the lofty seats of the Thrones; Thou wast far purer than any other creature; Through grace perfectly free from every stain of sin; Thy rank taketh precedence before the rank of the Principalities; Treasure of goodness; Unsurpassed in sanctity; Veiled glory in this lampless universe; Victor over the serpent; Victress in all God's battles; Virgin Mary, Mother of the Church; Whom all generations shall call blessed; Without equal among things created; Woman clothed with the sun; Woman on whose head is a crown of twelve stars, that is a crown of all the saints; Wonder of wonders; Wonderful woman; Worthy throne for the Divinity; A beginning to the restoration of heaven and the sanctification of the world; A creature infinitely pure and exquisite; A creature so lovable; A creature who was altogether a prodigy and a summary of wonders; A diligent pilgrim towards the heavenly and eternal city; A dwelling, the most illustrious for sweetness, for graces and for virtues; A faithful copy of the original; A force; a power for us, because she excels in lifting us; A frail and tender maiden; A friend to counsel thee; A fullness of innocence and holiness; A gift which only infinite love could have devised and given; A girl in contemplation bent; A graduate of the school for virgins in the temple of Jerusalem; A haven in all troubles and difficulties of body and soul; A heaven from the first of thy existence; A heaven that contains the Sun; A helper in need and tribulation; A holy place; A human being descended from Adam; A joyful sign to the Church of the answer to its constant prayer, "Come, Lord Jesus"; A listening girl encompassing the Word; A little and humble handmaid of God; A living and faithful reproduction of her most holy Son; A living image of Christ, our Redeemer and Master; A loyal servant of heaven; A martyr not by the sword of the executioner but by the bitter sorrow of her heart; A martyr in spirit; A martyr of patience; A mere creature in mortal flesh; A mere creature that has come from the hands of the Most High; A mighty champion who will defend us against all of the wiles of the evil one and guide us to her son; A militant in heaven; A militant who influences all men without exception; A most rich treasury in which he has laid up all that he has of beauty and splendor, of rarity and preciousness, including even his Own Son; A most wise teacher; A new creature from the heaven of the divine mind; A partner in the divine mysteries; A perfect example of a creature not only free from all taint of sin but also full of all grace; A perfect mold wherein we are to be molded in order to make her intentions and dispositions ours; A perfect setting for a perfect jewel; A physician, divinely mild and full of healing power; A pilgrim in the world; A place so high and so holy, which is guarded, not by one of the Cherubim like the old earthly paradise, but by the Holy Ghost himself, who is its absolute Master; A pledge, a security for our reconciliation with God; A pledge of God's love for us; A precious vase that held each day new offerings of blossomy; A priestess bearing the sacrament in loving veneration; A prodigy of humility; A protectress to shield thee; A rich harvest of grace; A salutary remedy; A seal upon my heart, because your love is as strong as death; A second Eve who brought forth Emmanuel; A secondary but universal meritorious cause of our supernatural life; A sign of motherly kindness, the living image of the mercy of God; A sinless creature and without measure superior to all the highest seraphim; A song of love inspired by the Holy Spirit; A soul that was pure and noble beyond all earthly measure; A special means of grace; A spouse so worthy and so amiable; A star thou art, which shinest with a radiance kind, upon each weary heart; A stronghold of God; A sublime example; A teacher and an instrument of divine wisdom; A teacher of the spiritual life for individual Christians; A throne of nobler gold, silver pure and queenly strong, His infinity to hold; A treasure; A vast abyss of humility and love; A wonder of physical and spiritual beauty; A work only surpassed by God; A world in herself; A world of marvels; A young maiden of the Temple of Jerusalem; Above all of the angels and saints; Abode of all divine graces; Above all those who have been outstanding in the world by their charms and attractions; Above the world, below thy Son; Abyss impenetrable; Acceptable above all creatures; Adjutrix; Administratrix of divine charismata; Administratrix of the sacrament of human rendemption; Admirable above others; Admirable creature; Admirable instructress; Admirable treasurer of God; Adorer of the Incarnate Word; After God, our supreme joy; After God, the most beautiful and the greatest marvel of the universe; All beautiful, and radiant with the utmost in human perfections; All blessed; All chaste; All fair,

O Mary; All fair to see, her robe of golden cloth, a robe of rich embroidery; All generations bless thee; All good; All gracious; All holy; All merciful; All mercy, all kindness; All nations recognize and praise thy grace and beauty; All perfect; All powerful in her intercession in obtaining pardon and succour for the unfortunate sons of Adam; All powerful with One Whom here on earth she greeted by the loving name of Son; All sweetness; All the grace of the way and the truth; All the saints are but rays of this sun, and streamlets flowing from this ocean; All worthy of praise; Almoner of all graces; Alone the chosen one and the perfect one; Altar and sanctuary; Always a militant; Always beautiful, always good, always strong; Amazingly beautiful and holy creature; Ambassadress; Amiable and courteous; Amiable and heavenly creature; Amiable and sublime creature; Amiable in the eyes of God, and of the angels and of the world; An abyss of graces; An enemy of pomp; An eternal thought of God; An everlasting glory; An example to all the rest of creation; An extraordinary union of graces; An invincible warrior in the defense of her servants; An object of delight for God and angels and men; An object of terror to the powers of hell; An ocean of greatness; An old world's fondest dream; An overflowing and inexhaustible vessel of grace; An unbounded power in the realm of grace; Angelic betrothed of Joseph, the just; Announced by the choir of prophets; Apostle par excellence of her Divine Son; Arbiter and dispenser of the treasures of God; Arbitress of our destiny; Archetype of purity and innocence; Archive of all the treasures of the Incarnate Word; Archive of grace; Assemblage of grace; Assistant of her divine Son; Associate in the labors of the Divine Redemption; Associate of the Redeemer; August princess; August sovereign; August temple of the most Holy Trinity; Aurora, source of purity; Bearer of light; Beautiful and full of grace; Beautiful and sweet in thy delights; Beautiful as the moon; Beautiful as the turtle dove; Beautiful beyond compare; Beautiful "dawn" which is always illumined with divine light; Beautiful gift of God; Beautiful in every way; Beautiful Jewish maiden; Beautiful love; Beautiful one; Beauty of Carmel; Beauty of the world; Begetter of reconciliation and of the reconciled; Beginning, middle and end of our felicity; Beginning of our salvation; Beloved and most loving mother; Beloved bride of the Holy Ghost; Beloved of angels; Beloved of God; Beloved of men; Beloved one of her Lord, loved more than all of the saints and angels together; Beloved spouse and mother; Benefactress of men; Benevolent neighbor to the women of Nazareth; Best human fulfillment of Christ's command "Be perfect as the Heavenly Father is perfect"; Beyond the saints who highest are, within the courts of heaven; Blessed among all creatures; Blessed and extolled of all nations; Blessed art thou more than all thy kind; Blessed art thou that hast believed, because those things shall be accomplished that were spoken to thee by the Lord; Blessed assurance; Blessed by the Holy Ghost by whose power you gave birth to the world's Savior; Blessed by the just because you hear their prayers, free them from temptation and increase grace in their souls; Blessed Dame in the high heaven; Blessed finder of grace; Blessed fountain, overflowing with unfailing joy; Blessed, free of blame; Blessed maid; Blessed of all generations; Blessed those who heard and kept the word of God, as she was faithfully doing; Blessed virgin, who by thy fiat hast saved a lost world; Blest are those who hear the word of God and keep it; Blest one; Blissful bearer of thy Maker; Blossom-crowned maiden; Breadth unspeakable; Breath of heaven; Bride of Christ; Bride of the Canticle; Bride of the Father; Bride of the Lamb; Bride of Yahweh; Bright mirror of all virtues; Brightness of Everlasting Light; Brilliant light of sanctity; Busy one of Paradise; By nature fairer, more beautiful and more holy than the Cherubim and Seraphim; By nature more beautiful, more graceful and more holy than the Cherubim and Seraphim themselves and the whole host of angels; Careful housewife of Nazareth; Careful teacher; Carrier of the olive branch; Cause of all blessings; Cause of joy in heaven; Cause of joy on earth; Cause of our joy; Cause of our salvation; Cause of universal joy; Celestial princess; Cellarer of the whole Trinity, for she pours out and gives the wine of the Holy Spirit to whomsoever she wills and to the extent that she wills; Champion of the divine faith; Channel of every grace which Jesus Christ has won; Cherished being; Chief miracle of God's omnipotence; Child bride; Child-bearing maiden; Child of Adam, the God-made father of the world; Child of virtue; Choicest blossom; Chosen among all creatures as the model of the new evangelical law and its Author; Chosen and beloved one among the children of Adam; Chosen and only one among creatures; Chosen before the ages; Chosen by the God of mercy to give to the world the Redeemer of the human race; Chosen dwelling-place of the Holy Spirit, his ciborium, his spiritual vessel; Chosen for the greatest sacrament of the divine Omnipotence; Chosen for the mother of the Only begotten; Chosen from the beginning; Chosen lady in whom our Lord found repose; Chosen mother of the divine Son; Chosen of heaven; Chosen one; Chosen treasure; Clean, pure, abounding in grace, and above all she is the mother of mercy; Closest of all creatures to God; Closest of all to God's heart; Clothed in variety; Clothed with divine grace as with a garment; Clothed with the purest gold of the Divinity; Clothed with the Sun, with crescent 'neath thy feet and the fair star-gems glistening in thy crown; Coadjutrix of Christ, our Lord; Coadjutrix of salvation; Coadjutrix of the admirable works and mysteries of our redemption; Coadjutrix of the Lord in his labors for the redemption of mortals; Co-helper in our redemption; Come over to me all of you that desire me, and you shall be filled with my fruits; Comely as Jerusalem; Commander-in-chief; Comandress of the Catholic faith; Companion and co-partner in the works of the redemption; Companion and helper of our Lord in his passion; Companion of the Redeemer; Compassionate and courageous; Compassionate heart of Mary Immaculate; Compassionate with the little and the poor; Completely without reproach; Conceived of the Spirit Holy; Conqueror of all heresy; Conqueror of evil and death; Conqueror of the infernal serpent from the first instance of thy existence; Consecrated to God; Cooperator in our justification; Cooperator with the Redeemer; Cooperator with your Son in the work of our redemption; Co-operatrix of the Incarnation; Co-priest; Co-redeemer, that is, the co-operator with Christ in the redemption of the world; Co-redemptress of the world; Co-redemptrix of the human race; Consolation of the saints; Consort in the work of our redemption; Consummate teacher; Counselor most venerable; Counselor of the world; Counterpart of Jesus, thy son; Courage of sinners; Court of the Eternal King; Co-worker of salvation; Creation's pride; Creator of poetry; Creature most pleasing and acceptable; Creature so pure and immaculate; Crown of all miracles; Crown of virginity; Crowned with sovereignty; Cure of hearts; Custodian and dispenser of all the graces which her divine Son merited for us through his death on Calvary; Custodian of all the treasures gained by her Son as God, on account of his infinite merits; Daily communicant at the Beloved Disciple's mass; Dear Madonna; Dear spouse; Deity's shrine; Delicate and tender maiden; Delight of all of the citizens of heaven; Delight of God the Father; Depository of the Divinity; Descendant of David; Descendant of the shepherdess Ruth; Disciple of Christ; Dispensatrix of all grace; Dispensatrix of all the treasures of heavenly grace; Dispensatrix of the treasures of the Divinity; Dispenser of all gifts without exception; Dispenser of all good things; Dispenser of all the goods which God grants to us miserable sinners; Dispenser of all the graces Jesus purchased by his death and by his Blood; Dispenser of divine mercy; Dispenser of God's graces; Dispenser of Our Lord's Blood; Dispenser of the gifts of God; Dispenser of the gifts of the Redemption; Dispenser of the merits of her Son; Dispenser of the treasures of heaven; Dispenser of the treasures of thy Son; Dispenser of the vast stores of heaven through her Son; Distinguished among the heavenly citizens; Distinguished and chosen among all creatures; Distributor of all graces; Distributor of every grace; Divine luminary; Divine oracle; Divine princess; Divine prodigy; Divine, triumphant princess; Dwelling-place of all the graces of the Most Holy Spirit; Dwelling place of light; Elect among creatures; Elect, exalted, powerful and full of the Holy Ghost; Elect of Almighty God; Elect of God Most High, to bear his Son and hers; Elect or chosen one of God; Elevated above the archangels; Elevated above the glory, above the honors which the saints possess, higher than the virtues, the benignity, the sweetness and charm of blessed spirits; Emblem of all that is good and pure; Eminently perfect; Empress and mistress of the militant Church, it's protectress, its advocate, its mother and teacher;

Empress of heaven; Empress of the Church; Empress of the starry sky; Empress of the world; Engendered from the fruitful race of patriarchs; Enthroned above the starry sky; Entirely beautiful and perfect; Entrusted with all of the treasures of God; Espoused wife of the Lamb; Eternally full of grace; Ethereal vision whose grace and valor have entirely subdued us; Ever spotless and ever blessed; Exalted above all of the works of God; Exalted above the angels; Exalted above the choirs of angels unto heavenly kingdoms; Exalted and blessed spouse; Exalted as the angels, patriarchs, prophets, apostles, confessors and virgins; Exalted in dignity according to the measure of his own Omnipotence; Exalted supereminently; Example of patience; Excellent masterpiece of the Most High; Exquisite example of retirement and modesty; Exquisite model whose virtues we must draw into ourselves; Exterminator of the enemies of God; Extremely kind and generous to all thy loving children; Exultant with joy; Fair and full of grace; Fair and gentle as the moon; Fair and most dear to God; Fair and royal; Fair and sweet; Fair dawn of destiny; Fair maiden, blessed from heaven; Fairest of the fair; Fairest one; Fairest pattern of maidenhood and maternity; Fairest thou where all are fair; Fairest woman-child e'er seen; Faithful and inseparable spouse; Faithful copy of her divine Son; Faithful handmaid of divine providence; Faithful harbinger of the springtime of grace; Faithful helper of her most holy Son; Faithful messenger; Faithful servant in the Church; Faithful spouse of the Holy Ghost; Far surpasses all other creatures both in heaven and on earth; Fashioned of flesh incorruptible; Filled with grace and gifts above those of the highest Seraphim of heaven; First in beauty as in power; First in watchings; Flame of wisdom; Fondest shepherdess; For all weary, thou art rest; Foreknown by the Most High and prepared for his work; Forerunner of the Son of Justice; Forth-bringer of the Ancient of Days; Forth-bringer of the Tree of Life; Fount of love and holy sorrow; Friend; Fruit of benediction; Fruitful spouse of the Holy Ghost; Full of every grace; Full of goodness to the just; Full of grace and consequently of love; Full of grace and all perfection; Full of grace, for grace is given to other saints partially, but the full plenitude of grace poured itself into Mary; Full of grace for herself; Full of grace for the sake of men; Full of grace, from which many small brooks flow, that moisten the earth, and water the garden of the world; Full of grace, virtue and the heavenly gifts; Full of liberality towards me; Full of light and grace and she bears within herself the Author of light; Full of love for us who are mortal; Full of the unction of mercy and of the oil of compassion; Fullness of all good; Fully attentive to the needs of others; General of the armies of God; Generator of charm; Generous to the needy; Gentle and full of grace; Gentle, chaste, spotless maid; Gentle maid of Galilee; Gentle maiden having lodged a God in her womb; Girl, empress and ruler; Glad creature; Glorified more than all others; Glorious example of humility; Glorious heaven; Glorious maid; Glory of Christians; Glory of Libanus; Glory of mankind; Glory of the Christian nations; God-bearer; God destined thee his chosen one and made thee mother of his Son; God great and powerful in this creature; Godlike creature; God's beautiful one; God's handmaid; God's handmaid full of every grace; God's handmaid low; God's holy spouse; God's lovely human bride; God's poor serving-child; God's pride and masterpiece; God's splendid marvel; God's treasure; Good, affable, compassionate and never tired of hearing the long complaints of the afflicted; Good Anna's promised child of Judah's royal line; Grace and sweetness; Gracious guest in Elizabeth's household; Gracious matron; Grand almoner of Divine Providence; Great chieftainess of the martyrs; Great militant; Great mistress of humility; Great princess; Great queen and teacher; Great sublime creature of God; Great teacher of humility; Greater than all heaven's throng; Greatest treasure of heaven and earth; Guarantee of our salvation; Guardian of the Emmanuel; Guardian of the heavenly mysteries; Guardian of the treasures of God himself; Guiltless in God's sight; Hail, full of grace; Hail Mary, of all things in this world most precious; Hail, O peace of God with men; Hallowed treasury for the wants of all creatures; Handmaid most perfect in God's sight; Handmaid of the Eucharistic Jesus; Handmaid of the Lord; Happy one; Happy parent, chose to bear thy Maker, God's eternal heir; Harbinger of peace; Harbinger of salvation; Haven in all troubles and difficulties of body and soul; He that harkeneth to me shall not be confounded; Health of the sick; Health of the world; Heaven declaring the glory of God; Heavenly commandress; Heavenly creature affluent with the delights of the Almighty; Heavenly instructress; Heavenly maid; Heavenly nurse; Heavenly patron; Heavenly physician; Heavenly princess Mary; Heavenly sovereign; Heavenly spouse; Heavenly teacher; Heavenly treasure; Heavenly treasurer of the Heart of Jesus; Heaven's delight; Heaven's light; Heaven's masterpiece, she will be after God our supreme joy; Height incomprehensible; Heiress of the grandeur of kings; Help of the abandoned; Help of the Church; Help of the helpless; Helper for every situation; Helper of all men; Helper of our redemption; Her highness; Her majesty; Her price is from afar and from the end of the earth; Her purity had ever been as spotless as that of the angels; Her will was always attuned to the will of God; Her womb God's citadel; Heroine; Hidden treasure of guilelessness; Highest in heaven but still lowly in heart; Highest sovereign; Holiest of all creatures; Holiest of all the holy; Holy and pure creature; Holy and singular; Holy and wonderful fruit; Holy both in body and spirit; Holy city; Holy in soul and in body; Holy maiden; Holy one; Holy spinner in the temple; Home of the homeless; Honor of all creation; Honored more fervently than all others; Honored with the dignity of pontiffs; Hostel of the Sun; Hostess; Humble handmaid of the Lord; Humble housekeeper; Humble in heart; Humble maid of Galilee; Humble princess Mary; Humble servant of God; Humblest of all creatures of God; Humblest of the humble; Ideal holiness; Illustrious exile in Egyptian land; Image of the humanity of Christ; Imitator of St. Ann's virtues; Immaculate in body and spirit, in faith and in love; Immaculate mirror of the Divinity, admitting no other image; Immaculate one, enclosed in your virginal flesh Him whom the whole world knows not how to contain; Immaculate, pure, blessed and holy above all creatures; Immaculate treasure-house of the Word of God; Immense treasury; Immortal almoner of graces; In her God was man and man was God; In her is the beauty of life; In her there was no disease to remedy and no stain to cleanse; In me is all grace of the way and of the truth; In mind and heart, she was most beautiful, spotless; so that never was there a woman like unto her; In the eyes of the mightiest King and his courtiers, excellest all that is not God in dignity and grandeur; In you are found gathered all good things; Inaccessible to venomous serpents; Incomparable in the charm of her beauty, nobility and grace; Incomparable loveliness; Incomparable mercy; Incomparable sanctity; Indicated by patriarchs; Industrious matron of the Holy Family; Ineffable miracle of the Almighty; Ineffable miracle of the Most High; Inestimable treasure; Inferior only to God and superior to all other creatures; Inquiring and contemplative; Inseparable companion of Jesus; Inspirer of beauty; Instructress and model; Instructress of holy Church; Intelligent; Intercessor of sinners; Inventrix of grace; Inviolate and altogether holy; Inviolate spouse; Isaiah's "Virgin (who) shall conceive and bear a Son whose name is God-with-us"; It is by thee every faithful heart is saved; Joined by an inseparable bond to the saving work of her Son; Joined to her Son's saving work on earth; Joy of heaven; Joy of our hearts; Joy of the humble; Joy of the just; Joy of the ransomed; Joy of the saints; Joy of the sick; Joy to all mankind, for redemption is nigh; Joy to the angels, for she is to be their queen; Joy to the Blessed Trinity, for she is to be the co-operatrix of the Incarnation; Joy to the saints for she is to be the mother of their Deliverer; Joy unto generation and generation; Keeper and dispenser of all the divine treasures; Kept safe by angels; Kind and loving; Kindest teacher and mother; Kingly throne; Kinswoman of God; Lamb-enthralled; Laughing shepherdess of cloudlets; Law of absolution; Leader and sovereign; Leaven of mercy, inducing the Most High to grant it; Legitimate and true teacher and superior; Length immeasurable; Liberal with the liberal and more liberal even than the liberal; Life-giver to posterity; Light of my soul when it is surrounded with darkness; Like a crystalline tablet on which was written the evangelical law; Like a dove brooding over the swelling waters; Like the fair tall columns of marble set upon bases of gold; Like the lowliest handmaid, who according to the word of David, keeps her eyes fixed upon the hand of her mistress, awaiting her commands; Lily-maiden; Lily of

Eden's fragrant shade; Living counterpart of her most holy Son; Living example; Living garden of Eden; Living image and faithful reproduction of Christ; Living image of his Divinity and humanity; Living image of the Only-begotten; Living light of holiness; Living proof of God's love for us; Lonely lady of Judea; Love-fount tender; Love most pure and sweet; Love of men; Loved more tenderly than all others; Loveliest maiden ever the Creator made; Loveliest one; Lovely beyond imagination; Lovely Jewess, the mother of Jesus; Lovely keeper of the stars; Lovely maid; Lover of purity; Lover of souls; Love's earthly bride; Love's great token; Loving princess; Lowly hand-maiden; Lowly maid of Nazareth; Lowly maiden of highborn race; Made much higher than the Cherubim and Seraphim; Madonna at Galloro; Madonna del Parto; Madonna ever hind; Madonna fair; Madonna of all the Americas; Madonna of music; Madonna of Nettuno; Madonna of the exiles; Madonna of the glen; Magnanimous soul; Magnificence of the Most High; Maid of destiny; Maid of Israel; Maid of matchless purity; Maid of Nazareth; Maid supremely blest; Maid who art crown'd above; Maid, who at that high call, with truth that match'd thine own humility, didst speak the "yes" the heavens would contemplate; Maiden all compassionate; Maiden blessed; Maiden, blest star; Maiden by whom the old fierce serpent mourns his loss for evermore; Maiden, chaste and pure; Maiden clothed in white virginity; Maiden fair; Maiden in whose blest womb the very Godhead worthily made stay; Maiden mild; Maiden so meek; Maiden sweet and holy; Maiden, the Father's spouse; Maiden whose holiness hath dazzled the heavenly armies; Maiden, with sorrow laden; Mainstay and groundwork of the Holy Church and of its founders, the Apostles; Majestic treasure of the whole world; Martyr of love and sorrow; Martyr of martyrs; Martyr of patience; Martyrdom's crown; Martyrdom's palm; Marvel of heaven and earth; Marvel of men; Marvel of the Lord; Marvel of the universe; Marvelous help of Christians; Mary enamoured of her divine Son; Mary shares in the authority of the Eternal Father over his Son's Humanity; Mary, the second heaven; Mary's womb, the treasury of the poor; Masterpiece of God; Masterpiece of grace; Masterpiece of the ages; Masterpiece of the Divine Artist; Masterpiece of the Most High; Masterpiece of the Wisdom of God; Matriarch ere any sea parted from the land; Merciful sovereign; Mercy-seat for the whole world; Mighty maid; Mildest of the mild; Minister of God; Minister of life; Minister of propitiation; Miracle ineffable; Miracle of purity, of love, of devotedness, of immense charity; Mirror of love; Modest-clean of heart; Modest spouse of a humble workman; More agreeable than the sunrise; More beautiful than the moon; More exquisite and admirable than the sun; More faithful than the angels in corresponding to divine grace; More glorious than Paradise; More holy than the Cherubim, the Seraphim and the entire angelic host; More lovely than the lotus; More pleasing to the Creator than the high heavens he made for his habitation; More powerful than all hell together; More powerful than all others as a means of uniting mankind with Christ; More pure and holy than the highest Seraphim; More pure than all the exalted spirits in heaven; More pure than the purest of angels; More valiant and powerful than the heavenly hosts of saints and angels; More wise and perfect in her deeds than the angels; More venerable than the symbolic ark of the covenant; Most amiable and gracious in the eyes of God and his creatures; Most amiable of creatures; Most beautiful and holy of all mere creatures; Most beautiful aurora, inflamed and refulgent as it were with the fiery clouds of the Divinity, which transformed all things within her; Most beautiful in countenance, most pure of heart and most holy in soul; Most blessed one; Most blessed soul; Most blessed spouse; Most chaste spouse; Most compassionate of all the compassionate; Most enlightened in your counsel; Most exact in ful-filling the divine law; Most excellent, most glorious, most holy and ever inviolate Virgin Mary; Most exquisite treasure of all the universe; Most faithful dispensatrix; Most faithful helpmate; Most faithful minister of Divine Providence; Most faithful of all creatures; Most faithful servant and friend; Most faithful witness and co-worker; Most glorious throne; Most gracious and liberal of all pure creatures; Most high, most humble one, above the world, below thy Son; Most high princess; Most highly exalted of all creation; Most holy and pure of all creatures; Most holy Mary, into whose hands He has pawned his Omnipotence; Most holy place; Most humble and pure princess; Most humble disciple; Most inflamed in your prayer; Most kind helper; Most loving spouse of the Holy Spirit; Most perfect and most holy of creatures; Most perfect disciple; Most perfect in every virtue; Most powerful and favored of all God's creatures; Most powerful and sympathetic of saints; Most powerful destroyer of heresy; Most powerful in your help; Most profound in humility; Most profound in your meditation; Most prudent creature; Most prudent spouse; Most pure and holy creature formed and conceived in the Divine Mind from the beginning and before all ages; Most pure and spotless creature; Most pure in soul and body; Most pure princess; Most sensitive in your compassion; Most serene empress; Most simple dove; Most sweet in her delights; Most vigilant sentinel; Most wise teacher; Most wonderful of God's creatures; Most worthy spouse; Most zealous princess; My body's healing; My counselor, sincere and true; My graceful chatelaine; My greatest security; My heart and my soul; My joy; My light; My love; My memory is unto everlasting generations; My most generous benefactor; My mother and my lady; My powerful sovereign; My sister, my spouse, is a garden enclosed, a fountain sealed up; My solace; My soul's saving; My sovereign; My strength; My support in my extreme misery; My sweetness and hope after Jesus; My teacher; My treasure; My whole life; Mysterious and godlike creature; Mysterious treasury dispensing unspeakable joy; Mystic church; Nature's recreation; Nature's restoration; New and wonderful work of the Most High; New joy of the saints; New phoenix; Next to God, the joy of the saints; No creature equals her; No creature ever loved as she; No creature in the world was so exalted as Mary, because no creature in the world ever humbled itself so much as she did; None can compare with thee; Not only placeless but also timeless in her love for all of us; Nourished by the holy descendants of priests; Nourisher of God and man; Novelty worthy of the Infinite Wisdom; Nurse of the new born Church; O blessed and most blessed; O heaven, greater and vaster than the heavens themselves; O joy unhoped for; O Mary, center of the whole world; Object of divine predilection; Object of our love; Object of terror to the powers of hell; Of all creatures the most amiable, the most beloved, the most loving; Of all creatures the most illumined; Of all God's creatures the most pure, most fair, most powerful; Of all my friends the best and dearest; Of earth, the fairest creature; Of mortals, honored most; Of purity, the crystal shrine; Offered to God as a sign of gratitude; Offspring of Adam; Omnipotent to save sinners; On her, as on the most noble foundation after Jesus Christ, rests the faith of all generations; One peerless mortal; One so singular among all creatures; One who, at our slightest sign, bends over us with a smile, alleviates our pain and wipes the tears from our eyes; One who follows us everywhere; One who was able to contain God; One whom the infinite God himself loves without bound or measure; One with all human beings in their need for salvation; Only and legitimate disciple of the Lord; Only one, elect as the sun; "Open Sesame" of God's own heart; Ornament and beauty of all the human race; Ornament of splendor of Carmel; Ornament of angels; Ornament of our Church; Our beloved; Our cardinal link with the Divine High Priest; Our chaste love; Our companion to eternal blessedness; Our constant company; Our co-redemptrix; Our counsel; Our counselor; Our deliverer; Our enlightener, who bore us a Light as a revelation to the nations; Our ever faithful messenger; Our heart's best love; Our leader and mistress; Our liberator from our calamities; Our life; Our Miriam; Our most charming princess; Our most kindly adviser; Our only and heavenly Phoenix; Our ordinary resource; Our perfecter; Our princess; Our proximate end; Our purifier, whose heart was pierced by Simeon's prophecy; Our race's most distinguished alumna; Our reconciliation and peace; Our reparatrix; Our salvation; Our shield; Our sister through ties of nature; Our solace in sorrow; Our support in every tribulation of life; Our sweetness; Our tainted nature's solitary boast; Our unfailing succor in trials; Our universal supplement with Jesus; Outstanding example of faithful service to God; Pacificatrix; Paradise of joy, for God overwhelmed her with the joy of grace; Paragon of chastity; Paragon of virginity and humility; Pardon of sinners; Participant in his dignity of Redeemer; Peace of God with men; Peerless creature; Peerless one among lovers for entertaining love without limitation of measure or manner; Peerless queen; Perfect and only one; Perfect contemplative; Perfect fulfillment of the will of God; Perfect image of the disciple of Christ, reflected every virtue and incarnated the evangelical beatitudes proclaimed by Christ; Perfect imitator of Christ; Perfect member of the early Church; Perfect militant; Perfect work; Perfection of justice; Perfectly beautiful in every way; Perfectly faithful to God; Perfectly holy; Perfectly redeemed in body and soul; Personification of "relativity" between man and God; Pinnacle of created perfection; Pinnacle of sanctity; Pledge of our pardon; Pledge of our salvation; Plenitude of sanctity; Portal and mediatrix of those who were to profit of the passion and the redemption of mankind; Portress dear; Possessed of all grace and beauty, without being wanting in any; Powerful princess of the heavens; Powerful rod with which the violence of the infernal enemies is conquered; Powerful vanquisher of all heresies; Preamble of the Christ; Precious child of earth; Prefigured and foretold by the prophets; Priest of the New Law; Princess of heaven; Princess of the heavenly court; Princess whom God's Spirit chose as bride; Princess whose beauty lured Love's kiss when life began; Privileged soul; Prodigy of holiness; Prop on which the Holy Church, now and during the ages in which it is to exist, shall rest securely in the midst of the persecutions and temptations of the enemies of the Lord; Prophetess; Propitiation for sin; Propitiatory or mercy-seat of the whole world; Protected by angels; Protector of the Son of God; Protectress; Prototype of the Catholic faith and of holy hope; Prudent and wise; Prudent dispenser of the plenitude of her graces and gifts; Prudent in the fashion of a noble mistress; Pure and chaste; Pure and stainless; Pure as a tower of ivory; Pure as mid-ocean spray; Pure as the mantling snow on Alpine crest; Pure as the milk-white dove that bathes in woodland spring; Pure as the Seraph's thought before the Almighty King; Pure as the snow; Pure as the summer sky; Pure creature, more holy, perfect and agreeable to his eyes than all those he had created or will create to the end of the world, or through the eternities; Pure in your life, like to a lamb; Pure lily-maid; Pure temple of the Holy Ghost; Purer and brighter than the chaste stars; Purer than the angels; Purer than the sun's rays; Pure stone; Purity personified; Radiant one; Radiant with purity; Raised above all things except God; Ransom of captives; Ready help in trouble's hour; Receiver of orphans; Reconciler of sinners; Reconciler of the whole world; Redeemer of captives; Redemptrix of souls; Remedy for all sorrows of the heart; Repairer of our calamities; Repairer of our fallen race; Repairer of the human race; Repairer of the lost world; Reparatrix of her parents; Reparatrix of the whole world; Residence of God; Resplendent more than all others; Resplendent with the purest sanctity; Responsive and creative; Rest from our mourning; Restoratrix of the human race; Restorer of peace and reconciler of enemies; Restorer of the lost world; Resurrection of those who fall; Rich and beautiful; Rich in mercy; Riches of the Deity; Rightly to be regarded as the way by which we are led to Christ; Root of our salvation; Royal maiden; Sacred heroine of the valiant people of Israel; Sacred maid; Sacred shrine of sinlessness; Safe response of men; Safeguard of the living; Safety of those who stand; Saint Mary of Mount Carmel; Salvation and expiation of the world; Salvation's fiat; Salvation's way; Sanctified in her mother's womb above all angels and saints; Sanctified soul; Second Eve; Secret love of the Eternal Father for the world; Secretary of the great counsel; Secure and most faithful depository; Seed not of enmity but of grace; Seraph of heaven; Servant and slave of the Lord; Servant of her vassals; Servant of the children of the Church; Set by God to be a vital element of his gracious scheme; Sharer in the work of man's redemption; Sharer of Christ's regal might; She, above all the saints, is most powerful to obtain whatever she wills; She being all love towards those whom she has thus adopted; She, being obedient, became the cause of salvation for herself and the whole human race; She bore the Everlasting; She bore the King Divine; She by herself has smothered and extinguished all the heresies of the whole world; She comes next to God; She cometh up from the desert flowing with delights, leaning on her beloved; She conceived the Son of God without the operation of man; She co-operated with Christ by her charity to give birth to the faithful in the Church who are members of the Head; She discovered salvation for all, and for her own sanctification; She found grace who brought forth the source of grace; She had begotten Eternal Life; She in whom the Deity itself finds so much pleasure and delight above all other creatures; She is concerned with the whole human race; She is easily found by them that seek her; She is like the merchant ship, she bringeth her bread from afar; She is universal-according to her own mode, which is to efface herself in Jesus; She knows no failures, what she seeks she finds; She merited for us in her subordinate way, all those graces which Christ has merited as the Head of the body; She next to God surpasses all in purity; She stands beside the right hand of her Son, Our Lord, the only-begotten Jesus Christ; She sums all virtues that may be; She that cometh forth as the morning rising, fair as the moon, bright as the sun, terrible as an army set in battle array; She, the primal seat of enmity, must never have any part with sin; She, who clothed her servants in double garments; She who extended her hands to the poor and opened her palms to the destitute; She who gave Him his rightful place in the very first Christian home; She, who girded herself with strength; She who has given to the world mercy in Jesus; She who nursed her Creator as an infant at her breast; She who obtains for those who attach themselves to her, the graces of fidelity to God and perseverance; She who put forth her arms to greater things; She who rises from the emptiness of this world, steeped in the delights of Paradise; She who together with her Maker recreates the human race, and redeems the souls of men by giving them her Son; She who was to be the habitation of the Son of God; She whom all the tongues of heaven and earth do not suffice to extol; She whose famous life still sheddeth lustre upon all the Churches; She whose heel is to crush the infernal serpent; She whose light was not extinguished in the night of tribulation; Shrine of the Divine Artificer; Shrine of the Holy Ghost; Shrine of the Trinity; Simple in your heart like a dove; Singular being; Singular consolation of all the holy souls in limbo; Sinless, rational creature; Sister and mother; So beautiful, so worthy and so perfect a spouse; So beautiful that when one has seen her, one can no longer love anything earthly; So delicate, yet so glorious; So gentle that Jesus can refuse her nothing; So mild, so merciful, so strong, so good; So modest and yet so mighty; So much has the Most High and powerful God favored this creature, that we, his angelic spirits, are full of astonishment; So patient, peaceful, loyal, loving, pure; So powerful with God; So simple and so lowly; So sublime in sanctity, that none but Mary was a fitting mother of God; So weak, yet so strong; Solace of our exile; Solace of the world; Sole and universal heiress of all the gifts of nature, of grace and of glory; Sole dispenser of his graces to ennoble, to exalt and to enrich whom she wishes; Sole repose of men; Solitary in her greatness amid his vast creation; Sorrowful spouse; Soul filled with a wisdom divine, in heart wedded to God; Soul, the most noble, the most pure that ever was, next to the soul of Jesus Christ; Source from which God's grandest graces spring; Source of every good; Source of immortal life; Source of joy; Source of mercy; Source of the Precious Blood; Source of true consolation; Source of our happiness; Sovereign above us; Sovereign benefactress; Sovereign, merciful and mild; Sovereign of all Christians; Sovereign of heaven and earth; Sovereign of the angels and of all the universe; Sovereign of the world; Sovereign princess, to whom all owe subjection in heaven and on earth; Sovereign spouse; Sparkling jewel of youth; Spiritual abode of the most spiritual souls; Spiritual paradise of God; Spotless bride; Spotless loveliness; Spotless maid, whose virtues shine with the brightest purity; Spotless mirror of God's majesty; Spotless mirror of justice; Spouse and servant of the Holy Ghost; Spouse, chosen among thousands; Spouse of Christ; Spouse of God; Spouse of St. Joseph; Spouse of the creative Spirit who renovates the nature of man; Spouse of Divinity; Spouse of the Eternal Spirit; Spouse of the Father; Spouse of the King; Spouse of the Lamb, that is Christ; Stainless maiden, springing from David's kingly line; Standard bearer of Christ; Standard for all men; Stands out among the poor and humble of the Lord; Star above the storm; Star-crowned; Stately prophetess of victory; Stay of widows; Store-house of God, filled with the everlasting joy of eternity; Storehouse of the treasures of heaven; Stranger among the children of Adam, captive in the bonds of mortal flesh; Strength of martyrs; Strong as a tower of David; Stronger than the earth, wider than the universe, for thou has conceived the God the world could not contain; Sublime and spotless; Sublime work of the divine omnipotence; Submissive in the manner of a humble servant; Sum and substance of the decrees of God; Sun of the Church; Sun without stain; Superabundantly filled with grace by the Holy Ghost; Superior in excellence and dignity to all creatures; Suppliant omnipotence; Supreme among mere creatures; Supreme empress and mistress of those caverns and dwelling-places of our enemies; Supreme glory of the tribe of Judah; Supreme mistress, mother, governess and sovereign of the Church; Sure pledge of redemption; Surest help to the knowledge and love of Christ; Surpassed all the martyrs in generosity; Surpassing Eden's Garden; Surpassing the heavens; Surpassing the Seraphim; Sweet and beautiful; Sweet as desert manna; Sweet as Eden's lilies; Sweet benediction in the eternal curse; Sweet charm of salvation; Sweet flowering of gracious mercy; Sweet fount of love; Sweet, loving and powerful to enrich our poverty; Sweet, lowly handmaid; Sweet modest little Nazareth flower; Sweet solace in pain; Sweetest of all creatures; Sweetest picture artist ever draw; Sweetest spouse; Sympathizer with the children of Eve; Tall Lady of the lilies; Teacher and example of all the believing; Teacher and guide of all the virgins and lovers of chastity; Teacher and mistress of all sanctity; Teacher in the doctrine of eternal life and salvation; Teacher of all sanctity and perfection; Teacher of all the creatures; Teacher of perfection; Teacher of prophets; Teacher of the Apostles; Teacher of the Church; Teacher of the holy Church; Teacher of virtues; Temple of the Holy Spirit; Tender maiden, full of grace and beauty; Tender spouse; Terrible to the devil and his crew, as an army ranged in battle; Terrible to the princes of darkness; Terror of demons; Terror of the proud; Testamentary executrix; That creature, in whom the human nature is freed from its first sin, who is to crush the head of the dragon; The assistant in the principal work for which the Incarnate Word came into the world; The astonishing virgin who ravished the vision of our wonderful prophet Isaiah; The aura of the Eucharist; The aurora sending forth the splendors of the Sun, Christ, true God and man; The beautiful one. my love, comely. slender and tall; The beautiful temple that was Mary's soul; The begetter of reconciliation and of the reconciled; The beginning of all our happiness; The beginning of perpetual life; The beginning of the warfare; The beginning, the middle and the end of our happiness; The beloved one; The best-beloved of the Most High; The best guide; The Blessed Virgin. our ordinary resource; The bride of the Dove; The bride, the wife of the Lamb; The bride whom the Father has espoused; The bright madonna; The brightest and dearest reflection of God's own holiness; The cause itself of joy; The cause of angel's jubilee; The cause of her own salvation and that of all mankind; The cause of the happiness of all men; The center and focus of all the wonders of the Almighty; The channel of that other outpouring of the Holy Spirit which formed the Church, the Mystical Body of Christ; The chaste spouse of the Holy Ghost; The cheer of those who vigils keep; The Cherub's glee; The chosen companion of Him who was to redeem the world; The chosen of all mankind; The crystal reflection of our Sun; The Church of the Living God; The dearest reflection of God's own holiness; The cloister garth which no man trod; The closest of all creatures to God; The companion for the ministry; The corn of heavenly bread; The counterpart of Eve; The creature excelling all others in dignity and grandeur above all understanding and calculation of the created mind; The dawn of grace; The delight of our eyes; The delight of the just; The depository and treasure-house of heavenly sacraments; The disciple of Christ; The disciple who is the active witness of that love which builds up Christ in people's hearts; The disciple who works for that justice which sets free the oppressed and for that charity which assists the needy; The divine world of God; The dream and the realization of all tenderness; The Eden of ancient, forgotten tenderness; The elect of Almighty God; The emancipator, Mary; The end of my captivity; The end of vices; The espoused wife of the Lamb; The exemplar for us of all Christian life; The fair glass and universal exemplar who shows us the way out of our darkness; The fairest flower of mankind; The figure of the synagogue; The finder of grace; The finest result of the redemptive work of her divine Son; The first after Jesus Christ, true God and true man; The first and most perfect disciple of Jesus Christ in the practice of all virtues; The first and peculiar work of God; The first and specially privileged disciple of her most holy Son; The first-born before all creatures; The first-born of God; The first Christopher, the first Christ-bearer; The first fruits of those who have fallen asleep; The first in God's design of the work of creation; The first object, out of all humanity. of the love of Christ; The first of mere creatures; The first, the highest and greatest of saints; The first to share from a full heart the joy that is Christ; The formal cause of our regeneration; The fragrance of that world unseen; The friend of mortals; The fullness of a fruitful life; The fullness of helping mercy; The fullness of illuminative wisdom; The fullness of overflowing grace; The fulfillment of prophecy; The future Eve, to whose offspring victory over Satan is promised; The general of the armies; The glorious foreshadowing of the eternal Son; The glory of angels; The glory of the heavens; The governess of heaven; The grand and divine world of God; The great and exclusive mold of God; The great missionary; The great queen and lady of all the universe; The greater Eve; The greatest among the lowly and poor of the Lord; The greatest glory of Christ because she has received the most from him; The greatest of all the martyrs; The greatest personal friend that Jesus had here on earth; The greatest treasure of the Divinity in the whole creation, next to the humanity of Christ, our Savior; The greatness of love; The guiding light for men journeying through life's tempestuous sea of temptation; The harbinger of peace and reconciliation; The hidden treasure of guilelessness; The hidden treasure of modesty; The heroine of the "Stabat," the "Mother of Sorrows"; The high mountain on which is to be established and constructed the new law of grace; The holiest, most authentic and happiest human being; The holy of holies where saints are formed and moulded; The holy one, and more glorious and pure, and more saintly than all the rest of human kind; The holy one of our race; The Holy Spirit's anguished bride; The honor and adornment of virgins; The honor of the human race; The honor of the earth; The humble maid immaculate; The humble maid of Nazareth; The humblest of all creatures; The ideal that fascinates us; The image and first flowering of the Church as she is to be perfected in the world to come; The ineffable; The inseparable companion of Jesus; The inspiration of prophets; The instrument and special dispensation of thy Son Jesus Christ; The instrument of the Holy Ghost; The instrument of the Incarnation; The instrument or the motive power through which the saints themselves have reached their station; The Jewish people's magnificent boast; The joy and fruition of the blessed; The joy of angels; The just men and kings bore witness to you; The keeper of the ineffable treasure of heaven; The law of clemency is on her tongue; The life of Christians; The life of our hearts; The light of earth, the sovereign of saints; The link between heaven and earth; The living image and portrait in everything of her divine Son; The living image of the mercy of God; The living mold of God; The living source of cleansing water; The Lord's humble handmaid; The loss that man in Eve deplores, thy fruitful womb in Christ restores; The love of my soul; The Madonna with her beautiful Babe; The magnificence of God; The magnificence of the Most High; The maid of the Annunciation; The martyr's palm by thee is borne; The marvel of God; The masterpiece beyond compare; The masterpiece of the hands of God; The masterpiece of the Holy Ghost; The means Our Lord made use of to come to us; The miracle of miracles of grace, of nature and of glory; The miracle of purity, of love, of devotedness, of immense charity which was the soul of Mary; The mirror reflecting all the thoughts, feelings, aspirations, desires and purposes of Jesus; The model, here below, in prayer; The mold of God; The most acceptable child of God; The most authentic form of the perfect imitation of Christ; The most beloved of God and his greatest lover; The most conformed of all creatures to Jesus Christ; The most excellent fruit of the redemption; The most exquisite treasure of all the universe; The most exquisitely formed image of Jesus Christ; The most generous and most grateful of creatures; The most perfect throne in all the world;

The most powerful and sympathetic of saints; The most precious, the most estimable and worshipful of all the creatures; The most pure of all creatures; The nations shall know her as the Blessed; The new Eve, who put her absolute trust not in the ancient serpent but in God's messenger; The noblest, the most exalted, the purest, the holiest of all things created; The obedient new Eve; The omnipotent answer to prayer; The one chosen by God to retain intact her virginity and yet also selected among all creatures as the mother of the Lord; The one creature, that could worthily intercede for sin and temper the wrath of the just Judge; The one full of grace; The one in whom the divine Word shall vest himself with human flesh and form; The one person whose virtue is unconquerable by the malice of Satan; The one who gave the world a God and King and called that God her son; The one who perfectly believed and hoped in all the mysteries; The only and legitimate disciple of the Lord; The only and worthy spouse; The only child of Adam who never for an instant bowed to the reign of Satan; The only hope of the Patriarchs; The only one and without a compeer among creatures; The only one without a peeress; The only Phoenix upon the earth; The only saint whose glorified body, like that of her Divine Son, does not have to await Gabriel's call to the fullness of life; The organ of the Holy Spirit and the representative of the Infant; The ornament of the heavens; The panegyric of all the ages and of all spheres; The paragon of maternity; The parent of salvation and of the saved; The patriarchs desired your birth, O Mary; The people of Israel sighed for you; The perfect Christian; The perfect example of creature holiness; The perfect example of the use of circumstances as a help to sanctity; The perfect one; The perfect type or representative of redemption in its very essence; The perfect victory of the grace of Christ in the weakness of the flesh; The person who encounters Mary cannot help but encounter Christ likewise; The personification of "relativity" between man and God; The place of delights; The plenitude of grace is thine; The powerful means of our redemption; The preparation for the Christ; The prodigy of grace and who has filled up the abysses of the guilt of all of the children of Adam; The prodigy of the divine perfections; The promise given to the Patriarchs; The pure beginning of all creatures; The purest and the most holy so that under God a greater purity cannot be understood; The purest, the fairest, the holiest of all things created; The rational paradise of the second Adam; The relation to God; The reminder that God loves us and we must love God; The representative of the believing remnant; The resting place of the Holy Trinity; The riches of my poverty; The rod of Jesse has blossomed; a virgin has brought forth him who is God and man; The royal princess of God, the King; The royal way of virgins; The sacred vine of divine wine; The safe and sure road to Christ, the star which leads us to him; The second or greater Eve; The secret of modesty; The scepter of orthodoxy; The Seraph's boast; The soul of blessed Mary. limpid clear as cloudless night, holds the Spirit of the Godhead in immensity and might; The source of the life by which we really live; The source of the Way, Life and Truth; The sovereign of the invisible world of spirits; The sphere of the omnipotence of God; The splendor of virtue; The spring that gives us purity; The spouse of the Divinity; The steadfast undoer of Eve's folly and our folly; The strength that fortifies our souls; The strong one who in her seed should conquer; The sublime creature dwelling on the confines of the Divinity; The superior of all creatures; The supreme among mere creatures; The sure means and the straight and immaculate way to go to Jesus Christ and to find him perfectly; The teacher and the mother of true wisdom; The throne of grace and true mystical propitiatory; The treasure of the Lord; The treasure, the treasurer and the dispenser of divine graces; The true Esther, most holy Mary; The truth revealed to the prophets; The type or figure of the virgin Church; The typical perfect believer; The unique militant; The utmost limit to which the love of Christ can proceed in mere creatures; The vastness of clemency; The vastest, the most efficient, the most universal supernatural power in heaven and on earth, outside the three Divine Persons; The very flood-tide of grace; The very heart of the Mystical Body; The very mercy of God; The very point in the whole history of our redemption at which the saving grace of the living God descends from him into this history; The very treasure of life; The village carpenter's wife; The way by which God has come to us; The way by which Jesus came to us the first time. she will also be the way by which he will come the second time, though not in the same manner; The way by which shall pass to men the various outpourings of his munificent goodness and omnipotence; The wise prophets announced you; The world of God; Theotokos (Mother of God); There is not in heaven nor on earth a creature worthy to be compared to you; They that explain me shall have life everlasting; They that work by me shall not sin; This fairest idea of God, whom no other so sweetly delighted; This maid supremely blest; Thou, after thy Divine Son, art the certain salvation of thy faithful servants; Thou alone hast destroyed all heresies in the whole world; Thou art become beautiful and sweet; Thou art exceedingly gracious; Thou art truly happy, O sacred virgin Mary and worthy of all praise; Thou at whose dear breasts the life himself drew life; Thou beauty; Thou canst not be thought of by those who love thee without filling their minds with joy; Thou gavest the world by human birth the most desired of heaven and earth; Thou harmony of nature's art; Thou hast all power to change hearts; Thou hast conceived the Creator of all creatures; Thou hast found grace with God-abiding grace; Thou hast found grace with God-all desirable grace; Thou hast found grace with God-everlasting grace; Thou hast found grace with God-exceeding grace; Thou hast found grace with God-greater than any other; Thou hast found grace with God-immovable grace; Thou hast found grace with God-invincible grace; Thou hast found grace with God-saving grace; Thou hast found grace with God-unfailing grace; Thou hast, in fact, far surpassed every creature; Thou hast ravished the gaze of the Adorable Trinity; Thou hast that Son as thy debtor, who gives to all and receives from none; Thou hast to the astonishment of nature given birth to the Creator; Thou living form among the dead; Thou lovest us with an invincible love; Thou mirror, in whom, as in the splendor of the sun, all shapes look glorious which thou gazest on; Thou of all creatures art the most noble, the most sublime, the most pure, the most beautiful, the most holy; Thou that bringest a joy that passeth not away; Thou that nourishes joy in the highest; Thou to the sorrowing here beneath hast opened heaven's eternal doors; Thou who, blessed by God, didst merit to bear the Redeemer of the world; Thou who didst bear the God-Man; Thou who dost aid the forlorn; Thou who hast placed in this world the Creator and Redeemer, our guide to the kingdom of heaven; Thou who sittest enthroned above all the choirs of angels, nearest to God himself; Thou who with neither toil nor sowing hast made the undying ear of corn to flourish; Thrice holy spouse; Throne, at which all—just and sinners—find the consolations of mercy; Throne of glory; Throne of His glory for His Father, because it is in Mary that Jesus Christ has calmed his Father, irritated against men; Throne of honor for the grandest princes of eternity; Throne of the heavenly King; Through thee every creature is rejoiced; Through thee, mankind obtains salvation; Through you are promised to us all delights; Thy fragrance is sweeter than all ointments; Thy garments are as white as snow and thy face like the sun; Thy handmaids are the daughters of princes; Thy instructress; Thy purity surpasses that of the angels and thy compassion that of the saints; Thy soul more purified than the finest gold; Treasure bright, of all delight; Treasure-house and channel of all graces which come to us; Treasure-house of life; Treasure-house of the Lord's graces; Treasure-keeper of heaven; Treasure of all holiness; Treasure of God, where He was pleased to put all He had most precious; Treasure of heaven and earth; Treasure of immortality; Treasure of the Lord; out of whose plenitude all men are made rich; Treasure of the world; Treasure worthy of veneration, that belongest to all mankind; Treasurer and dispenser of all the goods in heaven and on earth; Treasurer and dispenser of God's mercies; Treasurer and dispenser of the divine favors; Treasurer and dispenser of the gifts and graces of the Most High; Treasurer and universal dispenser of the merits and virtues of her Son; Treasurer of divine graces; Treasurer of God; Treasurer over the vast property of her Son, which is mercy, for God is mercy; Treasurer whose treasure is Jesus Christ; Treasury of all graces; Treasury of celestial gifts; Treasury of immortality; Treasury well nigh infinite; Tree that bears the Fruit of Life and the true mother who produces it; True model of meditation;

True Reparatrix; True spouse; Truly blessed one; Type of purity; Unbounded power in the realm of grace; Undefiled like a dove, all clean, all upright, full of grace and truth; Undefiled treasure of virginity; Unequalled and beloved treasure; Unique in the midst of the elect; Unique in the order of creation; Unique in your humility; Universal depositary of all our goods of nature and of grace; Universal dispenser of all divine graces; Universal dispenser of grace, the full and absolute disposal of the Eucharist and of the graces which it comprises; Unlearned in the ways of Eve; Untarnish'd by decay; Untouch'd by age; Utterly full of divine grace and loveliness; Vase of grace; Vast abyss of humility and love; Vastness of clemency; Vermilion rose of Trinity; Very treasure of life; Vessel of anguish; Victim for the human race; Victor in all of the battles of God; Victorious and triumphant mistress of angels and men; Victorious chieftainess; Victorious Sulamite; Virgin and immaculate earth, of which the New Adam was formed; Virginal spouse of the Christ Child's foster father; Virginal wisdom; Virtue rich and fruitful; Visage most resembling Christ; Vision of peace; Vision of the prophets; Vivifier of posterity; Wayfarer among the mortals; Wedded to God; Well-beloved of God; Well-beloved one; Well-beloved spouse; Well-spring of favors; White as untrodden drifts of Alpine snow; Who can never be loved according to her merits; Wholly and utterly, purity, kindness, love, faithfulness, patience, compassion and belongs to God alone; Wholly fair, wholly without sin; Whom all creatures should eagerly strive to love; Whom God himself declared of plenteous grace; Whom the angels love with all of their heavenly powers; Widow of Ephesus, perpetual Eucharistic adorer; Wife of Joseph, the carpenter; Wise and good counselor; Wise commander; With God, after God but under God, the efficient cause of our regeneration; With her grace none other e'er may compete here below or above; With the honor of virginity, Mary has the joy of motherhood; Within and without adorned in beauty; Without equal among things created; Witness of our toil; Wonder of the Most High; Wonderful and chosen creature; Wonderful being; Wonderful creature; Wondrous girl; Work of God; Workshop of the union of the natures; Worthy associate of the Redeemer; Worthy repairer of the lost world; Worthy teacher of the militant Church; You are beauty, la belta', and we cannot admire you enough; You are goodness, la bonta', and we cannot praise you enough; You are she who is always named, and you are she who cannot be named at her worth; You are the most great in your humility, the most beautiful in your virginity and the most ardent in your love, the most resigned in your patience; You give to the world the joy of its salvation; You have found grace even in the eyes of God; You, in whose maiden womb was formed long since in Galilee, the fairest of the sons of men; You merit all honor and glory; You preserve the honor of virginity; You who alone brought forth mercy by giving birth to Jesus; You who are so gentle and so compassionate to poor sinners; You who know how to give to the weak, strength, to the captive, freedom; Your firm support; Your superior and head; Zealous princess; Zelatrix of Jesus; A bridge of salvation; A guide in our youth; A helper for every situation; A secure means without delusion; A secure road which conducts to Jesus Christ and life eternal in a straight and secure manner; A short road which leads us to Jesus in a little time; A short road without danger; Adjutrix; An immaculate way without imperfection; Assured help of the miserable; Auxiliatrix; Certain pledge of my salvation; Certain salvation of Christians; Channel of all grace that flows from Jesus' Precious Blood; Channel of all our goods; Compassionate helper and deliverer; Direct road; Door through which sinners are brought to God; Established guide of poor mortals here below; Enlightened guide; Gate of life; Guide and protectress; Guide and teacher of the knowledge of Christ; Guide of confessors; Guide of the missionary; Guide of travelers; Guide of the wanderer; Heavenly chariot; Help of all who call on thee; Help of Christians; Help to the helpless; Helper in danger's dark hour; Helper of our salvation; Helper of sinners; Immaculate way; Ladder to Paradise; Link between heaven and earth; Loving aid in all our woes; Loving helper of the Christian people; Mankind's perpetual help; Means and custodian of our salvation; Means and negotiator of the salvation of all ages; Means of ascent to the heavenly kingdom; More powerful than all others to help us gain eternal life; My guide and counselor in this vale of tears; My guide in journeyings; My guide in the pilgrimage of this life; My soul's ladder and way to heaven; Our assistance in salvation; Our guide and our teacher; Our loving guide; Our ready help; Our safest way among life's turbulent waves; Parent of salvation and of the saved; Perpetual help; Portal of all the predestined; Portal of life and salvation for the sons of Adam; Powerful aid for help; Radiant bloom that lights life's lonely way; Regulator of our spiritual existence; Salvation of sinners; Salvation of all who call upon thee; Salvation of the dying; Salvation of the whole world; She does not disdain to serve those who serve her; Stewardess of every grace; Strength of all who stagger under burdens sore; Strength to the fearful; The channel by which Christ came to us; The channel of pardon; The road and the means to the end; The straight and secure way; The way of our salvation; The way to go to our Lord; A mediator in our behalf with Jesus Christ; Aqueduct of grace; Arbitratrix; Channel of grace; "Channel" or the "aqueduct" by which the waters of grace flow to man; Channel through which we receive all graces needful for our salvation; Ever-flowing channel of divine grace; Full of grace, not only for herself but for all men; In the communion of saints, she is the intercessor for all of us, the mediatrix of all graces; In the distribution of graces an "almost immeasurable power" was given to the Blessed Virgin Mary; Intermediary with the One who knows how to cure all things; Mary, in this position as intermediary, is entirely one of us, as a mere creature, to the one human family; Mediatress between heaven and earth; Mediatress between the judge and the culprit; Mediatress in grace; Mediatress in the salvation of mankind; Mediatress of all men; Mediatress of angels; Mediatress of peace between men and God; Mediatrix and sole advocate of this world; Mediatrix between God and man; Mediatrix of all graces; Mediatrix of mortals; Mediatrix of salvation; Mediatrix of the entire world; Mediatrix of those who turn to her for their salvation; Mediatrix to the Mediator; Mediatrix universal; Mediatrix with Christ, who alone is the Mediator; Mediatrix with the Son; Most faithful and powerful intercessor; Mysterious canal; Our go-between; Our mediatrix; Our mediatrix of intercession; Our mediatrix to the fullest extent possible to a mere creature; Our sovereign mediatrix with thy dear Son Jesus; Peace-maker between God and men; Powerful mediator; Reconciler of sinners; So powerful that none of her petitions has ever been refused; Special mediatrix of the human race; The immaculate way which leads us safe to the Heart of God; The most powerful and most sympathetic of all who mediate for us before God; The principal minister in the distribution of grace; Through whom all creation held fast by the madness of idolatry has come to the knowledge of the truth; Through whom angels and archangels are glad; Through whom churches are erected throughout the world; Through whom devils are put to flight; Through whom heaven rejoices; Through whom holy baptism has come to believers, and the oil of gladness; Through whom the apostles preached salvation to the nations; Through whom the dead are raised and kings reign; Through whom the fallen creature is taken up to heaven; Through whom the Holy Trinity is glorified and adored throughout the world; Through whom the nations are brought to repentance; Through whom the prophets foretold; Through whom the tempter-devil fell from heaven; Treasure-house and channel of all graces which come to us; Universal mediatrix and dispensatrix of all divine graces; Queen; Queen all unrivalled; Queen among sisters; Queen and advocate of us, miserable sinners; Queen and chief of martyrs; Queen and chief patronage dispenser of the merits of her Son; Queen and empress seated upon a royal throne; Queen and lady; Queen and leader of the white-robed virgins who, in heaven follow the Lamb whithersoever He goes; Queen and mistress enthroned at the right hand of herSon; Queen and mistress of all that is created; Queen and mistress of all virtues; Queen and mistress of angels; Queen and mistress of the Church; Queen and mistress of the humble; Queen and mother in the ancient land of Pompeii; Queen and mother of the Christian people; Queen and mother of us all; Queen and ravisher of hearts; Queen and sovereign; Queen and teacher of virtues; Queen at the right hand of thy Son; Queen beauteous and immaculate; Queen by the right of self-conquest; Queen, clothed in the gold of variety; Queen conceived without original sin; Queen crowned with twelve stars; Queen amid the horror and the agony of Gethsemane and Calvary; Queen exalted by heaven and earth; Queen forever; Queen glorified; Queen, glory of Carmel; Queen, immaculate, sublime; Queen in blue; Queen in golden raiment, wrought about with variety; Queen in Ophir arrayed; Queen Mary; Queen, model of adorers; Queen, most fair; Queen, most sweet; Queen, most worthy of love; Queen, mother and spouse of the King; Queen, not only because she is the mother of God, but also because, as the new Eve, she was associated with the new Adam; Queen of actors; Queen of all; Queen of all fair virtues; Queen of all flowers that light life's weary way; Queen of all hearts; Queen of all nature; Queen of all peoples; Queen of all priests; Queen of all saints; Queen of all that's fair in May; Queen of all the virgin choir; Queen of angels; Queen of apostles; Queen of believers; Queen of benignant grace; Queen of Carmel; Queen of charity; Queen of chastity; Queen of confessors; Queen of contentment; Queen of courtesy; Queen of creation; Queen of evangelists; Queen of every heart; Queen of every sanctity; Queen of gentleness; Queen of glory; Queen of heaven; Queen of heaven and earth; Queen of heaven and the lady ruler of the world; Queen of heaven enthroned; Queen of heaven's court; Queen of heaven's Seraphim; Queen of high estate; Queen of holy poverty; Queen of humility; Queen of immaculate birth; Queen of Ireland; Queen of joy; Queen of life; Queen of light; Queen of love; Queen of majesty; Queen of Marists; Queen of martyrs; Queen of May; Queen of men; Queen of mercy; Queen of mercy and mother of grace; Queen of mercy in the valley of Pompeii; Queen of mildness; Queen of militants; Queen of mothers; Queen of my heart; Queen of Nazareth; Queen of night; Queen of our grief and our pain; Queen of paradise; Queen of patriarchs; Queen of peace; Queen of peace and forgiveness; Queen of perseverance; Queen of Poland; Queen of prophets; Queen of purgatory; Queen of purity; Queen of queens; Queen of saints; Queen of salvation; Queen of sorrows; Queen of souls; Queen of surpassing greatness; Queen of tears; Queen of the Church; Queen of the Church suffering; Queen of the Church triumphant; Queen of the clergy; Queen of the communion of saints; Queen of the courageous; Queen of the court of God; Queen of the dolorous mysteries; Queen of the earth; Queen of the eternal years; Queen of the festival; Queen of the fount immaculate; Queen of the glorious mysteries; Queen of the heavenly court; Queen of the Holy Family's home at Nazareth; Queen of the human race; Queen of the Jews; Queen of the joyful mysteries; Queen of the kingdom of peace; Queen of the Legion; Queen of the missions; Queen of the Orders of Friars Minor; Queen of the peace that breathed at Nazareth; Queen of the rosary; Queen of the rosary in the valley of Pompeii; Queen of the seven sorrows; Queen of the shining host; Queen of the stars and stripes; Queen of the true faith; Queen of the world; Queen of victories; Queen of Viet Nam; Queen of virgins; Queen of virtues; Queen of zeal; Queen privileged above the laws of the children of Adam; Queen regent, because queen mother in the minority of her Son; Queen rich in mercy and magnificence; Queen seated at the right hand of the King; Queen since she brought forth a Son who, at the very moment he was conceived, was the Word, even as man, King and Lord of all things; Queen so sweet, clement, and so ready to help us in our miseries; Queen undefiled; Queen unrivalled; Queen, "who is always vigilant to intercede with the King whom she bore"; A queen of great power; Admirable queen; An ever gracious queen; Angel-queen; August queen of heaven; August queen of sorrows; August queen of victories; Beautiful, glorious, all-powerful queen of Ireland; Beloved Queen; Beloved queen in Paradise; Benign queen; Blessed queen; Blest queen of our hearts; Blissful queen; Bright queen of May; Celestial queen; Dearest queen; Devout queen; Earth and heaven's fairest queen; Ever humble queen; Exalted queen of all creation; Fairest Hebrew queen; Fairest queen; Faithful and thankful queen; Gentle queen; Glorious queen; Glorious queen of heaven and earth, in whom the Most Blessed Trinity is well pleased; Glorious queen of martyrs; Glorious queen of the most holy Rosary; Glorious queen of the world; God's queen; Gracious, gentle queen; Gracious queen of heaven and earth; Great and powerful queen; Great queen; Great queen and lady; Great queen and teacher; Great queen of heaven;

Great queen of humility; Great queen of the angels; Great queen of the world; Great queen, who wast assumed so royally into the kingdom of eternal peace; Great queen, who wast assumed to heaven most gloriously, in the company of souls drawn by thy merits out of purgatory; Hail holy queen; Heavenly queen; Heavenly queen, whose beauty surpasses that of all the angels and saints together; Heaven's bright queen; Holy Queen; Holy queen of humble hearts; Holy queen of souls; Humble queen; Immaculate queen; Immaculate queen, in whom all nations were to be blessed; Immaculate queen of peace; Invincible queen of heaven; Invincible queen of the angels; Jubilee queen; Lady queen; Legitimate and supreme queen; Loveliest queen; Lovely queen of peace; Magnificent queen and mistress of the heavens; Majestic queen of heaven; Mary, our queen; Mighty queen of honor and glory; Mistress and queen of the apostles; Mistress and queen of virtues; Most amiable queen; Most beautiful queen; Most compassionate queen; Most faithful queen; Most high queen of the universe; Most illustrious queen among all queens; Most innocent queen; Most kind queen of heaven; Most meek queen; Most prudent queen; Most pure and innocent queen; Most solicitous queen; Most sweet queen; Most truly queen; Most worthy queen of the universe; Most wonderful queen and mother; My cherished queen; My queen, most worthy of love; Noble queen; October's queen; Our beloved favor-bearing queen; Our blessed virgin queen; Our charming and beautiful queen; Our earthly queen; Our most kind queen and lady; Our most loving queen; Our most patient queen; Our princess; Our queen and advocate, who from the first instant of thy conception, didst crush the head of our enemy; Our queen is constantly before the divine majesty, interceding for us; Our queen most fortunate and blessed; Powerful queen; Pure queen; Queenly handmaid acquiescent to Gabriel's message; Radiant queen of love; Risen queen; Scapular queen; Sovereign of angels; Sovereign queen of all creation; Sovereign queen of the universe; Stainless queen; Supreme queen of heaven and earth; The Blessed Virgin (is our lady and queen because of the unique way in which she cooperated in our redemption; The blushing queen of blooms; The Church has honored her with the title of "Queen"; The first queen of the Catholic faith; The fortunate queen; The perpetual queen beside the King, her Son; The queen in a vesture of gold, wrought about with variety; The queen of Jalisco; The queen stood at thy right hand in golden vesture surrounded with beauty; The queen who brings peace; The world's majestic queen; Unconquerable queen; Virgin and queen of Pompeii; Holy Mary; Mother of God; Elect and predestined from all eternity; Daughter of God the Father; Mother of God the Son; Expected by the patriarchs; Foretold by the prophets; Desired by all nations; The joy of Israel; The glory of Jerusalem; Immaculate Conception; The new Eve; The purest, the fairest, the holiest of all things created; A pilgrim in the world; Angelic betrothed of Joseph, the Just; The blessed virgin; Our lady of Nazareth; Our lady of the Annunciation; The virgin who is to conceive and bear a son whose name will be called Emmanuel; Our lady of the visitation; Our lady of Bethlehem; Our lady of the nativity; Mother of the Infant Savior; Our lady of the presentation; Our lady of the purification; Illustrious exile in Egypt's land; Mother of the Crucified; Sorrowful mother; Stricken mother on Calvary's mount; Queen of martyrs; Mother of the Mystical Body of Christ, the Church; Our lady of the Cenacle; Queen of apostles; Widow of Ephesus, perpetual Eucharistic adorer; Daily communicant at the Beloved Disciple's mass; Our lady of the assumption; Our lady of the coronation; Queen of angels and men; Queen of the Church militant; Queen of the Church suffering; Queen of the Church triumphant; Mother of the Church; Mother of perpetual help; Advocate of sinners; Our intercessor and advocate at the hour of death and judgment; A sign of sure hope and solace for the Pilgrim People of God.

Subject Index

Scripture Index

John

Other Books By Dan Corner

The Believer's Conditional Security

Exhaustive (801 pages) ■ **Contemporary** ■ **Comprehensive** (195+ sources)
Fully documented (700+ footnotes) ■ **Fully indexed**
Historical, little-known facts

The Believer's Conditional Security is the most
exhaustive and comprehensive refutation to the once
saved, always saved (OSAS) teaching ever written. It
deals a deathblow to OSAS through a close examination
of the Scriptures, exposes the real John Calvin and
unmasks the Synod of Dort. Stanley, Swindoll,
MacArthur, Hunt, Hanegraaff, Ankerberg and many
others are quoted and refuted.

Softback or CD $19.50
Voice Book $24.50
Hardback $29.50
Call (724) 632-3210 for bulk discounts

$17.00 E-book
(E-book and CD are for PC only and require IE 4.0 or higher, obtainable free
from www.microsoft.com)

The Gospel According to Charles Stanley
This shocking and devastating exposé should be read by every professing
Christian. (42 pages)
$2.50 (Softback—Specify English or Spanish)
$2.50 Voice Book

$1.50 E-book
(E-book and CD are for PC only and require IE 4.0 or higher, obtainable free
from www.microsoft.com) **Call (724) 632-3210 for bulk discounts.**

Unmasking John MacArthur's
Calvinistic Version Of Saving Faith
This book reveals some of the inconsistent and unscriptural declarations of MacArthur's *holiness* teachings. (52 pages)
$5.95 (Softback)

A Critique Of Gail Riplinger's
Scholarship and KJV Onlyism
Loaded with shocking information. (54 pages)
$5.95 (Softback)

A Study On Biblical Salvation
This book will help to clear up the confusion that exists regarding the true way to enter the Kingdom. (54 pages)
$5.95 (Softback)

The Myth Of Eternal Security
This book includes 29 chapters that are articles by Dan Corner related to the subject of eternal security. A good volume supplementing our 801 page book, *The Believer's Conditional Security.* (191 pages)
$10.00 (Softback)